THE DEBT TO PLEASURE

THE DEBT TO PLEASURE

John Wilmot, Earl of Rochester,
in the eyes of his contemporaries
and in his own poetry and prose

edited by

John Adlard

FYFIELD BOOKS

A Carcanet Press Publication

For
MY MOTHER AND FATHER

aurum nostrum non est aurum vulgum

SBN 85635 091 5 – cloth
SBN 85635 092 3 – paper

First published in 1974
by Carcanet Press Limited
266 Councillor Lane
Cheadle Hulme, Cheadle
Cheshire SK8 5PN

Printed in Great Britain
by W & J Mackay Limited, Chatham

CONTENTS

'Tis not an easy thing to be entirely happy, but to be kind is very easy, and that is the greatest measure of happiness. I say not this to put you in mind of being kind to me; you have practised that so long that I have a joyful confidence you will never forget it; but to show that I myself have a sense of what the methods of my life seem so utterly to contradict.

Rochester to his wife

Introduction

THE credulous Dr Plot, author of *The Natural History of Oxford-shire*, once stood by some hayricks on the outskirts of Woodstock, testing an echo from 'the brow of the hill on which my Lord Rochester's Lodge stands'. Having read that Bacon had tried in vain to make an echo repeat the word 'Satan', he was delighted to find this echo 'neither so modest or frighted' of the Devil's name.[1] Many of his readers must have thought it only too natural that Echo should lose her inhibitions near that lodge where the diabolical Earl, with his diabolical friends from the court of Charles II, 'used the body' of more than one Woodstock girl, had 'lascivious pictures' drawn and ran out naked into the Park.

This diabolical, romantic Rochester has always been with us, together with the noble penitent of the other school of biographers, the merely wicked man converted on his death-bed, an example to us all. Probably nobody needs to be told that both versions are false. Yet little has been written on Rochester's character and poetry that brings out their true distinction. According to Dr Leavis, he 'had uncommon natural endowments which, it is reasonable to suggest, he might have done much more with had he been born thirty years earlier'.[2] There is little one can say with any certainty about what a man might have done had he been born into another age, but thirty years earlier the intellectual milieu would of course have been different, and it is Rochester's response to the intellectual milieu of the Restoration that brings him into harmony with certain thinkers who are changing our lives, or at least provoking us, today.

Wilhelm Reich has described 'what is called the cultured human' as 'a living structure *composed of three layers*':

On the surface he carries the artificial mask of self-control, of compulsive, insincere politeness and of artificial sociality. With this layer, he covers up the second one, the Freudian 'unconscious', in which sadism, greediness, lasciviousness, envy, perversions of all

7

kinds, etc., are kept in check, without however, having in the least lost any of their power. This second layer is the artifact of a sex-negating culture; consciously, it is mostly experienced only as a gaping inner emptiness. Behind it, in the depths, live and work *natural* sociality and sexuality, *spontaneous* enjoyment of work, *capacity for love*.[3]

To reach that 'third layer' one has not only to blast a way through the first; the terrors of the second have also to be encountered. Such was Rochester's Divine Comedy, with a coda including his dialogues with Burnet, preparatory to his conversion, and Robert Parsons' reading of the Suffering Servant, by which that conversion was effected. Anne Righter has described the conversion as the total collapse of a personality: his last letters and his recantation 'could have been written by anyone'; Rochester 'had effectively ceased to be Rochester'.[4] To Burnet he said, in those preparatory conversations,

the two maxims of his morality then were, that he should do nothing to the hurt of any other, or that might prejudice his own health: And he thought that all pleasure, when it did not interfere with these, was to be indulged as the gratification of our own natural appetites. It seemed unreasonable to imagine that these were put in a man only to be restrained, or curbed to such a narrowness. This he applied to the free use of wine and women.[5]

Burnet replied that 'if appetites being natural was an argument for the indulging them, then the revengeful might as well allege it for murder, and the covetous for stealing; whose appetites are no less keen on the objects; and yet it is acknowledged that these appetites ought to be curbed'. This can only be called a foolish answer, Rochester having defended pleasure provided it did 'nothing to the hurt of any other'. However, Burnet went on: 'If the difference is urged from the injury that another person receives, the injury is as great, if a man's wife is defiled, or his daughter corrupted . . .' and he makes it clear, later in his book, that these ideas of 'defilement' and 'corruption' were based not on love but on laws of property. 'Men', he says, 'have a property in their wives and daughters, so that to defile the one, or corrupt the other, is an unjust and injurious thing. . . .'[6] He proceeds from this to a negative view of the passions:

Why should we not as well think that God intended our brutish and sensual appetites should be governed by our reason, as that the fierceness of beasts should be managed and tamed by the wisdom, and for the use of Man? So that it is no real absurdity to grant that appetites were put into men, on purpose to exercise their reason in the restraint and government of them. . . .[7]

Burnet, then, sees as divinely ordained that Reichian 'artificial mask of self-control, of compulsive, insincere politeness and of artificial sociality', and the energies beneath wholly contemptible, mere sparring partners of Reason, to exercise and strengthen the 'first layer'.

Rochester, it seems, did not protest. 'All this he freely confessed was true. . . .'[8] But he was then a very sick man and we must compare these last conversations with his poetry and some part of its intellectual background. 'Sometimes', writes Burnet, 'other men's thoughts mixed with his composures, but that flowed rather from the impressions they made on him when he read them, by which they came to return upon him as his own thoughts, than that he servilely copied from any.'[9] Even so, Rochester read in Hobbes' _Leviathan_: 'There be also other names, called _negative_, which are notes to signify that a word is not the name of the thing in question; as these words, _nothing_ . . .,'[10] and wrote in his 'Upon Nothing':

> Great Negative, how vainly would the wise
> Inquire, define, distinguish, teach, devise
> Didst thou not stand to point their blind philosophies!

Here, though he told Parsons that Hobbes' philosophy 'had undone him, and many more,'[11] words rather than ideas are carried over,[12] naturally enough since Rochester was not a philosopher but a poet. The same is not true of another sentence in _Leviathan_: 'The _present_ only has a being in Nature; things _past_ have a being in the memory only, but things _to come_ have no being at all. . . .'[13] This became:

> All my past life is mine no more;
>   The flying hours are gone,
> Like transitory dreams given o'er

9

> Whose images are kept in store
>> By memory alone.

> Whatever is to come is not:
>> How can it then be mine?
> The present moment's all my lot, . . .

Time involves change. 'And because,' writes Hobbes in his sixth chapter, 'the constitution of a man's body is in continual mutation, it is impossible that all the same things should always cause in him the same appetites and aversions. . . .' Here is the background of the rest of Rochester's lyric:

> The present moment's all my lot,
> And that, as fast as it is got,
>> Phyllis, is wholly thine.

> Then talk not of inconstancy,
>> False hearts and broken vows;
> If I, by miracle, can be
> This livelong minute[14] true to thee,
>> 'Tis all that heaven allows.

Strephon, in an early dialogue-poem, had justified his jilting of Daphne by explaining that ''tis nature's law to change'. The task is to preserve humane behaviour in the face of this. Love is presented as a recurring death-wish, every orgasm being, in a stock seventeenth-century witticism, a death:

> When, wearied with a world of woe,
>> To thy safe bosom I retire,
> Where love and peace and truth does flow,
>> May I contented there expire,

> Lest, once more wandering from that heaven,
>> I fall on some base heart unblest,
> Faithless to thee, false, unforgiven,
>> And lose my everlasting rest.

If 'expiring' in one's mistress's arms was to Restoration readers a traditional joke (indeed, Dryden never tired of it), to Rochester it was also a very tender joke. 'Contented' on that 'safe bosom' he attains not only death but also 'everlasting rest' comparable to that, after death, for which the Christian hopes. The background seems to be in *Leviathan*, Chapter 2:

For men measure, not only other men, but all other things by themselves: and because they find themselves subject after motion to pain and lassitude, think every thing else grows weary of motion and seeks repose of its own accord; little considering whether it be not some other motion wherein that desire of rest they find in themselves consisteth.

In the continual 'motion', as Hobbes calls it in Chapter 1, 'of external things upon our eyes, ears and other organs thereunto ordained', the sensual women who move through men's lives play no small part. Hence Rochester's determinedly realistic view of love in a society where sex-negation and pornographic exploitation necessarily exist side by side. All that we can be sure of is the 'happy minute', the death which is both extinction and salvation, peace after orgasm, rest.

Ronald Berman sees Rochester's 'vision' only as 'a kind of ordering (no matter how absurd or obscene) of the existential in terms which life seems unlikely to provide'.[15] This seems to miss all that divine gusto. And Berman goes on: 'It deals with pleasure, but only as it is flawed and ambiguous. The profound sexuality with which it is expressed is loveless and rarely erotic.'

'Loveless' is no word to apply to 'Absent from thee, I languish still . . .', to the lines apparently addressed to the young actress Elizabeth Barry ('Leave this gaudy gilded stage'), to 'A Song of a Young Lady to her Ancient Lover', and to several more. Berman puts the Young Lady's lover in the same category as the hostess in 'Timon'. 'All,' he says, 'are images of the dead ideal.'[16] But the Young Lady, surely, is in love and happy. He forgets too – at least, he does not mention – that love between different generations is a standard Metaphysical theme.[17] In these poems Rochester has reached what Reich called the third layer: '*natural* sociality and sexuality, spontaneous enjoyment of work, *capacity for love*':

> Love, the most generous passion of the mind,
> The softest refuge innocence can find,
> The safe director of unguided youth, . . .

Love as a 'safe director' suggests that youth in love can do without moral guides. These are lines from a poem of Rochester's mature period, 'A Letter from Artemisia in the Town to Chloe in the Country', in which Artemisia complains that 'this only joy' has become 'an arrant trade', and lays the blame on her own sex:

> To an exact perfection they have wrought
> The action, love; the passion is forgot.

The result is a desperate battle for survival between the sexes, whether as wife or whore, husband or rake, demonstrated in the story of Corinna, later in the same poem. The victims of that battle are a deserted wife, a bankrupt husband, and another girl under the lash in Bridewell.

The 'natural sociality and sexuality' of Reich's 'third layer' undoubtedly endowed Rochester with both a 'spontaneous enjoyment of work' and a 'capacity for love'. His spontaneous enjoyment of the duties of a country landowner sets him apart from the other court wits, for whom, writes J. H. Wilson, 'the countryside was no more than a place of hideous banishment'.[18]

Even in those discussions with Burnet 'he slurred the gravest things with a slight dash of his fancy'. Like many another realist he chose to face the horrors of Reich's 'second layer' with brilliant clowning, defying without hesitation all taboos on subject or language. Exploding taboos he blasted his way through that cold crust, Reich's 'first layer'. 'Fair Chloris in a pigsty lay, . . .' begins a pastoral song; he complains that he has become 'a common fucking post'[19] and his mistress 'a passive pot for fools to spend in'[20] among people dedicated not to 'mere lust' ('there's something generous' in that, he remarks) but to the 'action' of love brought to 'an exact perfection', the passion forgot. Nowhere are taboos on word or subject rejected more emphatically than in the play *Sodom*. '*Sodom*, I assume, is spurious,' writes David Vieth,[21] and most people make the same assumption. But that assumption seems to be based on an article by Rodney M. Baine published as long ago as 1946.[22] Baine seems over-anxious that Rochester should be 'exculpated', should not be 'damned with *Sodom*', and his anxiety seems utterly out of place when we consider that other works confidently attributed to Rochester contain ideas and words quite as likely to be offensive.

And some of Baine's ideas are plainly silly. He tells us that *Sodom* 'contains a good deal of military characters and atmosphere', and that this makes one Fishbourne a more likely author, since he had been in the army, whereas Rochester had served his king only at sea. In fact there are no more military characters, no more military atmosphere, than in most heroic tragedies or heroic farces. It will probably never be known whether Rochester or Fishbourne or someone else wrote *Sodom*, but we may say at least there is no reason why Rochester should not have written it. There are some very spirited and funny passages. In the last years of his life Rochester set about 'altering' for the Restoration stage the old play *Valentinian* by Fletcher. Valentinian is a lecherous Roman emperor with a lecherous court; the name rhymes with Bolloximian (Bolloxinion in some manuscripts), who, in *Sodom*, is a lecherous king with a lecherous court. It seems just possible that Rochester diverted himself while at work on Fletcher's play by writing a quite uninhibited farce.

Rochester's interest in *Valentinian* is not hard to understand. In the tragedy of this late Roman emperor he could safely express his feelings on the reign of Charles II. From his boyhood there was a unique emotional link between him and the king; his father had saved Charles after the disaster at Worcester and died in exile in his service. Rochester had grown up without a father, and as he reached maturity Charles had not been slow to perform some at least of a father's offices, in financial help and the choice of a wife. Thus it is not surprising to find the well-known love-hate relationship between father and son. Generally Rochester treats the easy-going king with good-humoured banter, but at times he is contemptuous of a monarch who, as he puts it, may be controlled by anyone who knows how to play with his penis, and this contempt broadens into a hatred of all kings, 'from the hector of France to the cully of Britain'. This is the last line of the 'Satire on Charles II', in which he had seemed to approve the gentleness which dissociated Charles from the ruinous military adventures of Louis XIV. There is a similar judgement in a passage inserted in *Valentinian*:

> Yet even his errors have their good effects,
> For the same gentle temper which inclines
> His mind to softness does his heart defend

From savage thoughts of cruelty and blood.

There may be a connection with Rochester's drunken folly in the Privy Garden at dawn, when he smashed a set of dials after crying 'Dost thou stand here to fuck Time?' It has been said that the dials had a phallic appearance, but this is far from obvious in the drawing we have of them. Possibly Rochester was addressing not the mechanism but the painting of 'chaste, pious, prudent' Charles II adorning it. 'In His Majesty's picture,' we are told, 'the house is shown by the shade of the hour-lines passing over the top of the sceptre . . .',[23] and in the drawing we see Charles' rather phallic sceptre continually passing through Time. The king in *Sodom* declares that his penis shall be his sceptre. In the 'Satire' just quoted Charles' 'sceptre and his prick are of a length'. Samuel Pepys once made a similar observation. In short, to use our energies creatively and exultantly is the only effective response to the threat of Time, and there is more in life than copulation, especially for a king. According to another account of the smashing of the dials, Rochester quoted a well-known song by Shirley, a favourite of Charles, that tells us sceptre and crown must tumble down.

Rochester's critics still write gloomily of 'obscenity', but such laughter releases the dangerously repressed, and he knew that our passions are rivers refreshing or perilous depending on how we approach them:

> If any force
> Stop or molest them in their amorous course,
> They swell with rage, break down, and ravage o'er
> The banks they kissed, the flowers they fed before.[24]

Burnet writes of his 'strange vivacity'[25] and the 'two principles in his natural temper, . . . a violent love of pleasure and a disposition to extravagant mirth'.[26] This mirth seems to be missed by certain of his critics. 'Fair Chloris in a pigsty lay' is a gloriously funny poem, yet Anne Righter finds it 'horrifying' and the account of Chloris' rape (in her dream only) 'deprecating, brutal, matter of fact'. She devotes almost a page of heavy-handed analysis to what is simply a very good joke.[27] David Vieth on the same poem is even clumsier: it 'not only incorporates two planes of experience by being mock-pastoral as well as pastoral, but adds a third through its Freudian elements of wish-fulfillment in a dream and the symbolic cave with a gate at its mouth.'[28]

This 'extravagant mirth' sometimes moved him to 'go about in odd shapes, in which he acted his part so naturally that even those who were on the secret and saw him in these shapes could perceive nothing by which he might be discovered'.[29] The most famous of these 'shapes' was his disguise as Dr Bendo, the Famous Pathologist, under which name and title he practised Rabelaisian medicine and won great acclaim in the environs of Tower Hill. We are reminded of the conclusion to his 'Tunbridge Wells':

> Bless me! thought I, what thing is man, that thus
> In all his shapes, he is ridiculous?
> Ourselves with noise of reason we do please
> In vain: humanity's our worst disease.
> Thrice happy beasts are, who, because they be
> Of reason void, are so of foppery.

The same theme is pursued in 'A Satire against Reason and Mankind':

> Birds feed on birds, beasts on each other prey,
> But savage man alone does man betray.
> Pressed by necessity, they kill for food;
> Man undoes man to do himself no good.

The poem is based on the eighth satire of Boileau:

> Voit-on les loups brigands, comme nous inhumains,
> Pour détrousser les loups courir les grands chemins?
> Jamais, pour s'agrandir, vit-on dans sa manie
> Un tigre en factions partager l'Hyrcanie?
> L'ours a-t-il dans les bois la guerre avec les ours?

But the debt is wider – to the whole tradition of libertinism. 'Quant à la guerre . . .', wrote Montaigne in the *Apologie de Raimond Sebond*, 'il semble qu'elle n'a pas beaucoup dequoy se faire désirer aux bestes qui ne l'ont pas'. Montaigne frequently quotes Lucretius, and so do the libertines (in both the philosophical and merely sexual sense of the word) of Rochester's day. 'Besides,' declares the preface to the Lucretius translation published in 1682 by Thomas Creech of Rochester's college, Wadham, 'the admirers of Mr Hobbes may easily discern that his Politics are but Lucretius enlarged; his state of Nature is sung by our poet, the rise of laws, the beginning of societies, the criterions of just and unjust exactly the same, and natural consequents of the Epicurean origin of Man.' Several of Rochester's acquaintances – from Dryden, in a letter of 1673, to the author of a 'Prologue intended for *Valentinian*' – stress his love for Lucretius, which was evidently worth notice although shared at the time by a good number of educated, Epicurean people. Like Dryden, Evelyn and other contemporaries, he tried his hand at translating *De Rerum Natura*. Two fragments have come down to us, one of them the great invocation to Venus that opens Book One:

> Great mother of Aeneas and of Love,
> Delight of mankind and the powers above,
> Who all beneath those sprinkled drops of light
> Which slide upon the face of gloomy night,
> Whither vast regions of that liquid world
> Where groves of ships on watery hills are hurled
> Or fruitful earth, dost bless, since 'tis by thee
> That all things live which the bright sun does see.

Though Creech's translation appeared after Rochester's death, John Evelyn's was available to him:

> Rome's parent Venus, joy of Gods above
> And men, who under those bright signs that move
> In heaven, dost all comfort bring and mirth
> To the ship-bearing seas, corn-bearing earth,
> By thee conceived since all things living be
> Beholding the sun's light. . . .

Comparison with Evelyn's bald and literal version shows how richly Rochester has developed his original. Evelyn's first line is mere efficient translation, Rochester's has music and feeling. He has given new magic to the words Evelyn renders as 'bright signs', and the 'groves of ships' is his own startling phrase. However, the passage will not make sense unless we realize that 'whither' is a seventeenth-century variant of 'whether'. In the manuscript at Nottingham the three words after 'whither' have been substituted, in Rochester's hand, for a word that has been crossed out. David Vieth reads this as 'orbiting', which is not only unmetrical but impossible; the word was not used as a verb before this century. I believe Rochester wrote 'inhabiting'.

It is not difficult to understand Lucretius' appeal to the young Rochester: he combines a determination to free mankind from unreasonable fears, to teach it to see things as they are, with a delight in the fruitfulness of Nature, whose genial power he invokes as Venus. To men of many ages he has given tranquillity of mind. But not, alas, to Thomas Creech, who, according to Hearne, was 'a very proud, morose, sour man' and, ignoring Lucretius' advice on love, hanged himself because a mistress was unkind.

We have already noticed the quest for tranquillity, for rest, in Rochester's poetry. We may be glad that at last he found rest in God as Robert Parsons read to him of the Suffering Servant in Isaiah. What is sad is to see him surrendering, in his sickness, to a second-rate debater like Burnet. Earlier he had begun long and serious discussions with a more attractive figure, Charles Blount, who believed that 'the passions were given to be used', that 'when Reason has examined the object, to consider whether it be good or evil, pleasant or painful, it has done its office and leaves the passions to exert their force, sets 'em no bounds'. I quote from the 'Account of the Life and Death of the Author' prefixed to his *Miscellaneous Works* of 1695, an account which continues:

He had been bred in a just and adequate notion of the Deity; he had learned that God was the first Cause of all things, was One and Indivisible, was Goodness itself, infinite and uniform in all his attributes; and held that we have a true and perfect knowledge of what is meant by Goodness, Justice, Mercy, Unity, &c. since else we could never know that God was good, just, merciful, one &c. This was his test of all doctrines, and when he met with such as opposed any of these Divine attributes or made them oppose one another, he rejected them as false and impious. He not only embraced evident truths in his own mind, but like a sincere lover of truth endeavoured to promote it, to disabuse the deceived and establish a pious and just notion of the Eternal Source of the Good-

17

ness, Wisdom, Power, Justice and Mercy. A noble task, and worthy his heroic spirit. But the Age was too corrupt. . . .

With such a friend, it seems to me, Rochester might have arrived at conclusions more in keeping with the experience of a lifetime, the experience of a man who (ironically, in Burnet's words) was 'a Master indeed, and not a bare trifler with wit . . .' one 'qualified . . . to have been one of the most extraordinary men not only of his nation but of the age he lived in'.[30] In the composite biography that follows the reader will find sufficient evidence to judge the truth of this for himself.

All spelling has been modernized. This was David Vieth's policy in the most recent and best edition of Rochester and seemed to me a sensible course, because this book is meant for a great variety of readers.

Punctuation has been modified where I felt understanding was impeded.

1

'Those Shining Parts . . . Began to Show Themselves'

1647   *1 April*. John Wilmot born at Ditchley manor house, Oxfordshire, to Henry Wilmot, Baron Wilmot of Adderbury, Royalist general, and Anne, daughter of Sir John St John.

1652   *13 December*. Father created Earl of Rochester.

1655   *February, March*. Father led abortive Royalist rising in Yorkshire.

1657/8   *19 February*. Father died in exile.

1659/60   *18 January*. Rochester matriculated at Wadham College, Oxford.

1660   *25 May*. Charles II, restored, landed at Dover.

1660/1   *February*. King granted Rochester a pension in gratitude for his father's loyalty.

1661   *21 November*. Rochester left England for a tour of France and Italy with Sir Andrew Balfour.

1664   *Christmas Day*. Rochester, returned from his travels, appeared at court with a letter to the king from his sister, the Duchess of Orleans.

His Birth and Parentage

John Wilmot Earl of Rochester was born in April, Anno Dom. 1648. [*sic*] His father was Henry Earl of Rochester, but best known by the title of the Lord Wilmot, who bore so great a part in all the late wars that mention is often made of him in the History: And had the chief share in the honour of the preservation of His Majesty that now reigns, after Worcester Fight, and the conveying him from place to place, till he happily escaped into France: But dying before the King's return, he left his son little other inheritance but the honour and title derived to him, with the pretensions such eminent services gave him to the King's favour: These were carefully managed by the great prudence and discretion of his mother, a daughter of that noble and ancient family of the St Johns of Wiltshire, so that his education was carried on in all things suitably to his quality.

Gilbert Burnet, *Some Passages of the Life and Death of the Right Honourable John Earl of Rochester*, London, 1680, pp. 1–3

His Birthplace in Oxfordshire

(i)

Hence we went to Ditchley, an ancient seat of the Lees, now Sir Hen: Lee's, a low, ancient timber house, with a pretty bowling green: My Lady gave us an extraordinary dinner: This gent: mother was Countess of Rochester, who was also there, & Sir Walt: Saint Johns: There were some pictures of their ancestors, not ill painted; the Gr: grandfather had been knight of the garter, also the picture of a Pope & our Saviour's head. . . .

John Evelyn, *Diary*, 20 October 1664

(ii)

So I walked a mile & an half through a very pleasant country, in a good measure adorned with marvellous pleasant woods, till I came against Ditchley House, about a furlong on the west hand of the road. As soon as I entered in at the great gate I observed an old ditch running directly by the house, & on each side planted with trees, which are very thick. . . . As I was gazing at this ditch & admiring the situation of the house, which is placed on the side of a hill, . . . I espied an elderly man going to work. I took the opportunity to ask him the name of this ditch. *Why, Master*, says he, *this*

is Grim's Ditch, & it runs on through the Park & so on to Charlbury,
Cornbury and Ramsden, where it joins with the Akeman Street. . . .

This old house is a very notable thing, & I think I was never better pleased with any sight whatsoever than with this house, which hath been the seat of persons of true loyalty & virtue. The front on the south side is very pretty, considering the method of building at that time.

We passed through the kitchen & came into the great Hall, which is above 9 yards in length, & is eight yards & an half in breadth. I was mightily delighted with the sight of this old Hall, & was pleased the more because it is adorned with old stags' horns, under some of which are . . . inscriptions on brass plates, which are the only inscriptions I ever saw of the kind. . . . I saw this date (1592) upon one of the leaden spouts of the house. The house itself was built before that year. But I cannot tell how old it is. It seems to have been done in the time of K. Hen. VIII.

10 June 1718; *Remarks and Collections of Thomas Hearne*, VI, Oxford, 1902, pp. 187, 188, 192

His Tutor

Mr Giffard tells me that he was tutor to the Earl of Rochester (mad Rochester) before he came to Wadham College, which was in the eleventh year of his age, and that he was then a very hopeful youth, very virtuous and good natured (as he was always) and willing & ready to follow good advice. He was to have come to Oxford with his Lordship, but was supplanted. His Lordship had always a very good opinion of Mr Giffard. Mr Giffard used to lie with him in the family, on purpose that he might prevent any ill accidents. . . . Mr Giffard says that my Lord understood very little or no Greek, and that he had but little Latin, & that therefore 'tis a great mistake in making him (as Burnet & Wood have done) so great a master of classic learning. He said my Lord had a natural distemper upon him which was extraordinary, & he thinks might be one occasion of shortening his days, which was that sometimes he could not have a stool for 3 weeks or a month together. Which distemper his Lordship told him was a very great occasion of that warmth and heat he always expressed, his brain being heated by the fumes and humours that ascended and evacuated themselves that way.

16 November 1711; *Remarks and Collections of Thomas Hearne*, III, Oxford, 1889, p. 263

At Burford Grammar School

(i)

⌈Anthony Wood tells us that he was 'educated in grammar learning in the free school at Burford, under a noted master called John Martin'. Since in 1673 this John Martin, in a friendly reply to Christopher Wase of Oxford, who was making a survey of grammar schools, transcribed the 'Constitutions' of the school without comment, we may suppose that these rules were as applicable in Rochester's day as they were when drawn up by one Simon Wysdom in 1571.⌉

Every scholar to pay 4d. entrance fee and 2d. a quarter. Everyone that comes out of the country to pay 12d. entrance and 6d. a quarter, except benefactors, and they to pay 4d. entrance and 2d. a quarter. The scholars to go to school at 6 o'clock in the summer and 7 in winter, and stay till 11 o'clock, and return from dinner at 1 o'clock in winter, and stay till 6 o'clock in summer and 4 o'clock in winter, and go to church with their Master; and, if there are no prayers, to sing psalms and to read a chapter in the school.

Schoolmaster every Sunday to appoint his scholars to come to his house by 8 of the clock in the morning to say prayers and to go with the Master to church. The Master four times a year to exhort the scholars to give thanks to God and recite the names of all the Founders and Benefactors, whose names to be written in a table to be put up in the School House, and then sing a psalm and depart from the school.

Simon Wysdom, *Constitutions*, 1571

(ii)

When he was at school he was an extraordinary proficient at his book: and those shining parts which have since appeared with so much lustre began then to shew themselves: he acquired the Latin to such perfection that to his dying-day he retained a great relish of the fineness and beauty of that tongue: and was exactly versed in the incomparable authors that writ about Augustus's time, whom he read often with that peculiar delight which the greatest wits have ever found in those studies.

> Gilbert Burnet, *Some Passages of the Life and Death of the Right Honourable John Earl of Rochester*, London, 1680, p. 3

'Wadham College in Oxford'

(i)

As for his education, it was in Wadham College in Oxford, under the care of that wise and excellent governor Dr Blanford, the late Right Reverend Bishop of Worcester; there it was that he laid a good foundation of learning and study, though he afterwards built upon that foundation hay and stubble.

> Robert Parsons, *A Sermon Preached at the Funeral of the Rt Honorable John Earl of Rochester*, Oxford, 1680, p. 6

(ii)

. . . became a Nobleman of Wadham Coll. under the tuition of Phineas Bury, Fellow, and inspection of Mr Blandford, the Warden, *an.* 1659, actually created Master of Arts in Convocation, with several other noble persons, *an.* 1661; at which time, he, and none else, was admitted very affectionately into the fraternity by a kiss on the left cheek from the Chancellor of the University (Clarendon) who then sate in the supreme chair to honour that assembly.

> Anthony Wood, *Athenae Oxonienses*, II, London, 1692, cols. 488, 489

(iii)

It was therefore, some space after the end of the Civil Wars, at Oxford, in Dr Wilkins his lodgings, in Wadham College, which was then the place of resort for virtuous and learned men, that the first meetings were made which laid the foundation of all this that followed. The University had at that time many members of its own who had begun a free way of reasoning and was also frequented by some gentlemen of philosophical minds whom the misfortunes of the Kingdom and the security and ease of a retirement among gown-men had drawn thither. . . . By this means there was a race of young men provided, against the next age, whose minds, receiving from them their first impressions of sober and generous knowledge, were invincibly armed against all the enchantments of enthusiasm.

Thomas Sprat, *History of the Royal Society*, 1667

(iv)

When he went to the University the general joy which over-ran the whole nation upon his Majesty's Restoration, but was not regulated with that sobriety and temperance, that became a serious gratitude to God for so great a blessing, produced some of its ill effects on him: He began to love these disorders too much; his tutor was that eminent and pious divine Dr Blanford, afterwards promoted to the sees of Oxford and Worcester: And under his inspection, he was committed to the more immediate care of Mr Phineas Berry, a Fellow of Wadham College, a very learned and good natured man, whom he afterwards ever used with much respect, and rewarded him as became a great man.

Gilbert Burnet, *Some Passages of the Life and Death of John Earl of Rochester*, London, 1680, p. 3

(v)

[The young Earl 'began', as Burnet put it, 'to love these disorders too much' in the company of Robert Whitehall, Fellow of Merton, whom Anthony Wood describes as a 'useless member' of that college. Some years later he addressed a verse-letter, with his portrait, to Rochester.]

My Lord,
Our picture we have sent,
An emblem of approaching Lent:
But that red letter in each cheek
Speaks Holyday, not Ember Week:
So incorporeal, so airy
This Christmas 'twill be ta'en for fairy.
Hang it or burn it, choose you which.
Yet now I think on't 'tis no witch,
Nor conjuror, for (to its grace)
You'll find it has no Bacon face:
And though orbicular the frame
It bears a more majestic name.

　　Hang it, but have a care lest [ ]
M[ay] seek to espouse it to Q: M[ab]
That would be what the Greek calls φοβερον
To come to Court to prave K: Oberon.
'Tis not in vest, but in that gown
Your Lordship daggled through this town
To keep up discipline and tell us
Next morning where you found good fellows.

　　Were I but worthy to advise
My Lord, you should in any wise
Place me directly over right
Your close-stool, so that at midnight
When you come in from play at Court
From masque or ball or such like sport
You may by looking on your friend
Need no foocatt, nor candle's-end.

　　If with acceptance you befriend it
　　'Tis for a New Year's gift intended.
　　Since Janus then two faces had,
　　Accept of ours, though ne'er so b[ad].

Postscript.

> Omnia cū frigent friget et ingeniū.
> When all things round about us freeze
> Wit is not fine, but on the lees.

My dearest Lord.
Yr. honrs. most entirely devoted.
Ro: Wh:ll.

M : C : Oxoñ.
Jan: 1 $\frac{66}{67}$

Nottingham University, Portland MSS., Pw V502

Abroad with Dr Balfour

(i)

But the humour of that time wrought so much on him, that he broke off the course of his studies, to which no means could ever effectually recall him till when he was in Italy his governor Dr Balfour, a learned and worthy man, now a celebrated physician in Scotland his native country, drew him to read such books as were most likely to bring him back to love learning and study: and he often acknowledged to me, in particular three days before his death, how much he was obliged to love and honour this his governor, to whom he thought he owed more than to all the world, next after his parents, for his great fidelity and care of him, while he was under his trust. But no part of it affected him more sensibly than that he engaged him by many tricks (so he expressed it) to delight in books and reading: so that ever after he took occasion in the intervals of those woeful extravagancies that consumed most of his time to read much: and though the time was generally but indifferently employed, for the choice of the subjects of his studies was not always good, yet the habitual love of knowledge together with these fits of study, had much awakened his understanding, and prepared him for better things when his mind should be so far changed as to relish them.

> Gilbert Burnet, *Some Passages of the Life and Death of the Right Honourable John Earl of Rochester*, London, 1680, pp. 4–6

[Years after, Balfour, 'a man of an excellent wit, and of a ripe judgement, and of a most taking behaviour,' wrote a book on travel in France and Italy. He nowhere mentions Rochester, but their itinerary together must have been very much like this.]

I suppose you leave Paris about the beginning of June (for I would not have you lose the month of May in the King's Garden, in regard most things will be then, or a little before, in their prime, which now that the Garden of Blois is no more in condition, is undoubtedly the best you are like to meet with) and therefore, 1. you may go to Orleans by the Messenger: it is but two days' journey; lodge *Chez Monsr. Ogilbie, sur l' Estape au Roy de la Grand Bretaigne;* a day or two will serve you to see all that is considerable in the place; it will be worth your while to see a place some two leagues from the city, called the Source, where in the midst of a fair green meadow you will see a spring of water so plentiful that it is navigable from its head and pours out a river called Loirette. 2 ly. From Orleans to Blois they count 15 leagues, yet it is but a short day's journey: besides, if you please, you have the commodity of the river to go by boat; be pleased to take notice of a place by the way, some 4 leagues from Blois, called St Die, where the best claret in that country grows, and is ordinarily to be found. Blois of itself is no very considerable town, yet it is famous for making of watches, for the civility of the people, for the sweetness of the air, and purity of the French language. You must stay there some days till you have seen the following particulars; *viz.* in one day you may get to Chambort, a house belonging to the King, some three leagues off, on the south side of the river, and south-east from the town; it is said to have been built by King Francis I and is a very stately house, though of a far different order of architecture than what is now used. From thence you may go to Herbeau, 3 leagues to the southward of that, a private house belonging to a gentleman that bears the title thereof. It is a very pleasant seat having very fine gardens with an orangery, fish-ponds, woods, maille and meadows belonging to it; from thence you may go to Beau Regard, another private house, where amongst other pretty things, you will see a fine gallery well ornamented with the pictures of such persons as have been illustrious for some age; from thence you return to Blois at night, & as you go and come you will have occasion to see that part of the forest of Blois that lies to the south of the river and town; as also a little village called St Gervais, famous over all that country for excellent cream. . . .

From hence you go to Venice by water, that is in an open boat, by a canal near to the side of the Po, where ye imbark in a bigger vessel, which goes constantly twice a week to Venice. If the wind be favourable, you will easily accomplish the voyage in 10 or 12 hours' time, but if otherways, you may be longer, and therefore you will do well to make provision of victuals, to take along with you. When you arrive at Venice, it will be needful to lodge in a convenient place of the town, and for that end, you will do well to provide yourself of a recommendation to the English Consul; from Rome or from Bologna. Giles Jones was Consul in my time, and entertained lodgers himself; he was a very honest man and did faithfully send my things to London, according to the address I gave him. When you are settled in a lodging, it will be time to take a view of the town, for the doing of which and considering it well, 3 or 4 weeks is little enough. Nothing in Nature can appear more prodigious than to see a vast big town seated in the middle of the sea; every house whereof at one side or another is touched by the water, and the nearest land being 4 or 5 miles distance. It was built at first upon the little island of Rialto in the year 421, perhaps later, by the inhabitants of the firm land that were chased from their own homes by Attila King of the Huns, & forced to make choice of this place for their safety; since that time they have built upon 70 or 71 isles more, which are joined together by upwards of 450 bridges. . . .

Although a traveller cannot be altogether sure of his times, there being so many contingencies that may force him either to arrive too soon or too late; yet it were to be wished that a man might happen to be at Venice in the time of Carnival, because of the operas and fine shows that are to be seen, and the extraordinary music at that time. In the summertime the great divertisement is to go in gondol upon the Great Canal, where towards the evening one may see five or six hundred gondols touring up and down, full of ladies and gentlemen, & several of them with music, both vocal and instrumental; which is one of the greatest gustos imaginable.

You cannot miss to meet with a great many curiosities here, both natural and artificial, because of the great resort that strangers have to this place, especially from the Levant; you will find medals, intaglios, cameos &c. amongst the goldsmiths. I have seen several curiosities to sell in the Place of St Mark, and sometime within the Court of the Palace, and in many other corners throughout the city. You may meet with many curiosities of glass that are both useful and delightful. It will be worth your while to visit the booksellers' shops, for besides many curious books that you may light upon here, and particularly of botany, you may likewise find very many books that are prohibited in many other places of Italy. Be pleased to inquire diligently for a thin 4° called *Trattato de simplici Pietre. & pesci marini che nascono del lito di Venetia di Antonio Donati Farmacopeo all' insegno di St Liberale in Venetia 1631*. Printed by Pietro Maria Beriano. Donati himself was dead before I came thither, but I found out his brother, a man of the same profession and living at the same place, but nothing knowing in simples. After I had told him the respect I had for his brother's memory and my regrate for the loss of so worthy a person, he was pleased to show me a great many brass plates of so many plants not yet described, together with their description done by his brother; I am confident were they published, they would make a bigger volume than the first.

Sir Andrew Balfour, *Letters Write to a Friend*,
Edinburgh, 1700, pp. 20–2, 214–16, 225–7

2

'Many Wild and Unaccountable Things'

1665	*25 May*. Rochester attempted to abduct Elizabeth Malet, Somerset heiress. Sent to the Tower.
	10 June. Plague reported in the City.
	19 June. Rochester released from the Tower.
	29 June. Court left London because of the Plague.
	15 July. Rochester joined the Fleet.
	16 September. Back at court, reporting to the king on the engagement at Bergen.
1666	*20 July*. Briefly rejoined the Fleet. In action five days later.
	2–5 September. Great Fire of London.
1666/7	*29 January*. Rochester married Elizabeth Malet.
1668/9	*16 February*. Boxed Tom Killigrew's ears in the king's presence.
	12 March. Travelled to France to deliver a letter for the king but also to avoid public indignation. Remained until July.
	30 August. Baptism of his first child, Anne.
1670/1	*2 January*. Baptism of his son, Charles.

'A Strange Vivacity of Thought'

(i)

He came from his travels in the 18th year of his age, and appeared at Court with as great advantages as most ever had. He was a graceful and well shaped person, tall and well made, if not a little too slender: He was exactly well bred, and what by a modest behaviour natural to him, what by a civility become almost as natural, his conversation was easy and obliging. He had a strange vivacity of thought and vigour of expression: His wit had a subtility and sublimity both, that were scarce imitable. His style was clear and strong: When he used figures they were very lively, and yet far enough out of the common road: he had made himself master of the ancient and modern wit, and of the modern French and Italian as well as the English. He loved to talk and write of speculative matters, and did it with so fine a thread, that even those who hated the subjects that his fancy ran upon, yet could not but be charmed with his way of treating of them. Boileau among the French, and Cowley among the English wits, were those he admired most. Sometimes other men's thoughts mixed with his composures, but that flowed rather from the impressions they made on him when he read them, by which they came to return upon him as his own thoughts, than that he servilely copied from any. For few men ever had a bolder flight of fancy, more steadily governed by judgment, than he had. No wonder a young man so made and so improved was very acceptable in a Court.

> Gilbert Burnet, *Some Passages of the Life and Death of the Right Honourable John Earl of Rochester*, London, 1680, pp. 6–8

(ii)

Afterwards he travelled into France and Italy, and at his return frequented the Court (which not only debauched him but made him a perfect *Hobbist*).

> Anthony Wood, *Athenae Oxonienses*, II, London, 1692, col. 489

Two Encounters

(i)

My Lord Rochester attempting to kiss the Duchess of Cleveland, as she was stepping out of her chariot at Whitehall Gate, she threw him on his back, and before he rose he spoke the following lines.

> By Heavens! 'twas bravely done,
> First to attempt the Chariot of the Sun
> And then to fall like Phaeton.

The Miscellaneous Works of the Right Honourable the Late Earls of Rochester and Roscommon, III, London, 1707, p. 135

(ii)

As a proof of his wit, the following is recorded: Meeting Lord Rochester one day at court, his lordship, by way of banter, thus accosted him: 'Doctor, I am yours to my shoe tie.' Barrow, seeing his aim, returned his salute as obsequiously, with 'My Lord, I am yours to the ground.' Rochester, improving his blow, quickly returned it with 'Doctor, I am yours to the centre'; which was as smartly followed by Barrow, with 'My Lord, I am yours to the antipodes': upon which Rochester, scorning to be foiled by a musty old piece of divinity (as he used to call him), exclaimed, 'Doctor, I am yours to the lowest pit of hell!' on which Barrow, turning on his heel, answered, '*There*, my lord, I leave you.'

British Museum Add. MS. 19, 117, f. 61, (Davy MSS.) notes on Isaac Barrow

The Abduction of Elizabeth

(i)

About 18, he stole his lady, [Elizabeth] Malet, a daughter and heir, a great fortune; for which I remember I saw him a prisoner in the Tower about 1662.

John Aubrey, *Brief Lives*

Thence to my Lady Sandwich's, where, to my shame, I had not been a great while before. Here, upon my telling her a story of my Lord Rochester's running away on Friday night last with Mrs Mallet, the great beauty and fortune of the North, who had supped at Whitehall with Mrs Stewart, and was going home to her lodgings with her grandfather, my Lord Haly, by coach; and was at Charing Cross seized on by both horse and footmen, and forcibly taken from him, and put into a coach with six horses, and two women provided to receive her, and carried away. Upon immediate pursuit, my Lord of Rochester (for whom the King had spoke to the lady often, but with no success) was taken at Uxbridge; but the lady is not yet heard of, and the King mighty angry and the Lord sent to the Tower. Hereupon my Lady did confess to me, as a great secret, her being concerned in this story. For if this match breaks between my Lord Rochester and her, then, by the consent of all her friends, my Lord Hinchingbroke stands fair, and is invited for her. She is worth, and will be at her mother's death (who keeps but a little from her), £2,500 per annum. Pray God give a good success to it!

Samuel Pepys, *Diary*, 28 May 1665

Two Naval Battles

(i)

Soon after his coming thither he laid hold on the first occasion that offered to shew his readiness to hazard his life in the defence and service of his country. In Winter 1665 he went with the Earl of Sandwich to sea, when he was sent to lie for the Dutch East India Fleet; and was in the *Revenge*, commanded by Sir Thomas Tiddiman, when the attack was made on the port of Bergen in Norway, the Dutch ships having got into that port. It was as desperate an attempt as ever was made: during the whole action, the Earl of Rochester shewed as brave and as resolute a courage as was possible: a person of honour told me he heard the Lord Clifford, who was in the same ship, often magnify his courage at that time very highly. Nor did

the rigours of the season, the hardness of the voyage, and the extreme
danger he had been in, deter him from running the like on the very
next occasion.

Gilbert Burnet, *Some Passages of the Life and Death
of the Right Honourable John Earl of Rochester*,
London, 1680, pp. 8–10

(ii)

From the coast of Norway amongst the rocks
aboard the *Revenge*.
August the 3rd. [1665]

Madam,

I hope it will not be hard for your Ladyship to believe that it
hath been want of opportunity and no neglect in me the not writing
to your Ladyship all the while. I know nobody hath more reason to
express their duty to you than I have, and certainly Savill [would]
never be so imprudent as to omit the occasions of doing it. There
have been many things past since I writ last to your Ladyship. We
had many reports of De Ruyter and the East India Fleet but none
true till towards the 26 of the last month we had certain intelligence
then of 30 sail in Bergen in Norway, a haven belonging to the King
of Denmark. But the port was found to be so little that it was im-
possible for the great ships to get in, so that my Lord Sandwich
ordered 20 sail of fourth and fifth rate frigate to go in and take them.
They were commanded by Sir Thomas Tiddeman, one of the Vice-
Admirals. It was not fit for me to see any occasion of service to the
King without offering myself, so I desired and obtained leave of my
Lord Sandwich to go with them and accordingly the thirtieth of this
month we set sail at six a clock at night and the next day we made
the haven Cruchfort (on this side of the town fifteen leagues) not
without much hazard of shipwreck, for (besides the danger of rock
which according to the seamen's judgement was greater than ever
was seen by any of them) we found the harbour where twenty ships
were to anchor not big enough for seven, so that in a moment we
were all together one upon another and ready to dash in pieces,
having nothing but bare rocks to save ourselves in case we had been
lost; but it was God's great mercy we got clear and only that we had

no human probability of safety; there we lay all night and by twelve a clock next day got off and sailed to Bergen full of hopes and expectation, having already shared amongst us the rich lading of the East India merchants, some for diamond[s], some for spices, others for rich silks and I for shirts and gold, which I had most need of; but reckoning without our host we were fain to reckon twice. However, we came bravely into the harbour in the midst of the town and castles and then anchored close by the Dutchmen. We had immediately a message from the Governor full of civility and offers of service, which was returned by us, Mr Mountegue being the messenger; that night we [had] 7 or ten more, which signified nothing but mere empty delays. It grew dark and we were fain to lie still until morning. All the night the Dutch carried above 200 pieces of cannon into the Danish castles and forts and we were by morn drawn into a very fair half moon ready for both town and ships. We received several messages from break of day until four of clock much like those of the over night, intending nothing but delay that they might fortify themselves the more; which being perceived we delayed no more but just upon the stroke of five we let fly our fighting colours and immediately fired upon the ships, who answered us immediately and were seconded by the castles and forts of the town, upon which we shot at all and in a short time beat from one of their greatest forts some three or four thousand men that were placed with small shot upon us; but the castles were not to be [taken] for besides the strength of their walls they had so many of the Dutch guns (with their own) which played in the hulls and decks of our ships that in 3 hours' time we lost some 200 men and six captains, our cables were cut, and we were driven out by the wind, which was so directly against us that we could not use our fireships, which otherwise had infallibly done our business; so we came off having beat the town all to pieces without losing one ship. We now lie off a little still expecting a wind that we may send in fireships to make an end of the rest. Mr Mountegue and Thomas Windham's brother were both killed with one shot just by me, but God Almighty was pleased to preserve me from any kind of hurt. Madam, I have been tedious, but beg your Ladyship's pardon who am

Your most obedient son,
ROCHESTER

I have been as good a husband as I could, but in spite of my teeth have been fain to borrow money.

British Museum, Harleian MS. 7003

(iii)

When he went to sea in the year 1665, there happened to be in the same ship with him Mr Mountague and another gentleman of quality; these two, the former especially, seemed persuaded that they should never return into England. Mr Montague said he was sure of it: the other was not so positive. The Earl of Rochester and the last of these entered into a formal engagement, not without ceremonies of religion, that if either of them died, he should appear and give the other notice of the future state, if there was any. But Mr Mountague would not enter into the bond.

When the day came that they thought to have taken the Dutch Fleet in the port of Bergen, Mr Mountague, though he had such a strong presage in his mind of his approaching death, yet he generously stayed all the while in the place of greatest danger: The other gentleman signalised his courage in a most undaunted manner till near the end of the action, when he fell on a sudden into such a trembling that he could scarce stand: and Mr Mountague going to him to hold him up, as they were in each other's arms, a cannon ball killed him outright and carried away Mr Mountague's belly, so that he died within an hour after. The Earl of Rochester told me that these presages they had in their minds made some impressions on him, that there were separated beings: and that the soul, either by a natural sagacity or some secret notice communicated to it, had a sort of divination: But that gentleman's never appearing was a great snare to him during the rest of his life. Though when he told me this, he could not but acknowledge it was an unreasonable thing, for him to think that beings in another state were not under such laws and limits that they could not command their own motions but as the Supreme Power should order them: and that one who had so corrupted the natural principles of Truth, as he had, had no reason to expect that such an extraordinary thing should be done for his conviction.

Gilbert Burnet, *Some Passages of the Life and Death of the Right Honourable John Earl of Rochester*, London, 1680, pp. 16–19

(iv)

For the summer following he went to sea again, without communicating his design to his nearest relations. He went aboard the ship commanded by Sir Edward Spragge the day before the great sea-fight of that year: Almost all the volunteers that were in the same ship were killed. Mr Middleton (brother to Sir Hugh Middleton) was shot in his arms. During the action, Sir Edward Spragge, not being satisfied with the behaviour of one of the captains could not easily find a person that would cheerfully venture through so much danger, to carry his commands to that captain. This Lord offered himself to the service; and went in a little boat, through all the shot, and delivered his message, and returned back to Sir Edward: which was much commended by all who saw it. He thought it necessary to begin his life with these demonstrations of his courage in an element and way of fighting, which is acknowledged to be the greatest trial of clear and undaunted valour.

Gilbert Burnet, *Some Passages of the Life and Death of the Right Honourable John Earl of Rochester*, London, 1680, pp. 10, 11

Rochester at a Ball

I also to the ball, and with much ado got up to the loft, where with much trouble I could see very well. Anon the house grew full, and the candles light, and the King and Queen and all the ladies set: and it was indeed, a glorious sight to see Mrs Stewart in black and white lace, and her head and shoulders dressed with diamonds, and the like a great many great ladies more, only the Queen none; and the King in his rich vest of some rich silk and silver trimming, as the Duke of York and all the dancers were, some of cloth of silver, and others of other sorts, exceeding rich. Presently after the King was come in, he took the Queen, and about fourteen more couple there was, and begun the Bransles. As many of the men as I can remember presently were, the King, Duke of York, Prince Rupert, Duke of Monmouth, Duke of Buckingham, Lord Douglas, Mr Hamilton, Colonel Russell, Mr Griffith, Lord Ossory, Lord Rochester. . . .

Samuel Pepys, Diary, 15 November 1666

Rochester Married to Elizabeth

Soon as dined, my wife and I out to the Duke's playhouse, and there saw 'Heraclius', an excellent play, to my extraordinary content; and the more from the house being very full, and great company. . . . Here I saw my Lord Rochester and his lady, Mrs Mallet, who hath after all this ado married him; and, as I hear some say in the pit, it is a great act of charity, for he hath no estate. But it was pleasant to see how everybody rose up when my Lord John Butler, the Duke of Ormond's son, come into the pit towards the end of the play, who was a servant to Mrs Mallet, and now smiled upon her, and she on him.

Samuel Pepys, Diary, 4 February 1666/7

Letters to His Wife

(i)

From our tub at Mrs Fourcaud's this 18th of October [1669]

Wife, our gut has already been griped and we are now in bed, so that we are not in a condition of writing either according to thy merit or our desert. We therefore do command thy benign acceptance of these our letters in what way soever by us inscribed or directed, willing thee therewithal to assure our sole daughter and heir issue female, the Lady Anne, [part] of our best respects; this, with your care and diligence in the erection of our furnaces, is at present the utmost of our will and pleasure. . . .

'Tis not an easy thing to be entirely happy, but to be kind is very easy, and that is the greatest measure of happiness. I say not this to put you in mind of being kind to me; you have practised that so long that I have a joyful confidence you will never forget it; but to shew that I myself have a sense of what the methods of my life seem so utterly to contradict. I must not be too wise about my own follies, or else this letter had been a book dedicated to you and published to the world: It will be more pertinent to tell you that very shortly the King goes to Newmarket, and then I shall wait on you at Adderbury: In the meantime think of anything you would have me do, and I shall thank you for the occasion of pleasing you. . . .

It is now some weeks since I writ you word that there was money returned out of Somersetshire for your use, which I desired you to send for by what sums yourself pleased. By this time I believe I have spent it half; however, you must be supplied if you think fit to order it; shortly I intend to give you the trouble of a visit, 'tis all I have to beg your pardon for at present, unless you take it for a fault that I still pretend to be

> Your humble servant,
> ROCH.

I do not know if my mother be at Ditchley or Adderbury; if at home present my duty to her.

I have, my dear wife, sent you some lamb, about an ounce; I have sent to my mother one Westphalia ham, one jole of sturgeon; and on Christmas Day I will send her a very fat doe. I fear I must see London shortly, and begin to repent that I did not bring you with me; for since these rakehells are not here to disturb us you might have passed your devotions this Holy Season as well in this place as at Adderbury. But, dear wife, one of my coach-mares is dying, or I had sent my coach instead of my compliment.

Yours, etc:

ROCHESTER

(v)

Newmarket.

I'll hold you six to four I love you with all my heart. If I would bet with other people I'm sure I could get two to one, but because my passion is not so extensive to reach to everybody, I am not in pain to satisfy many, it will content me if you believe me and love me.

ROCHESTER.

British Museum, Harleian MS. 7003

Two Principles

He had so entirely laid down the intemperance that was growing on him before his travels, that at his return he hated nothing more. But falling into company that loved these excesses, he was, though not without difficulty, and by many steps, brought back to it again. And the natural heat of his fancy, being inflamed by wine, made him so extravagantly pleasant, that many to be more diverted by that humour, studied to engage him deeper and deeper in intemperance: which at length did so entirely subdue him; that, as he told me, for five years together he was continually drunk: not all the while under the visible effect of it, but his blood was so inflamed, that he was not in all that time cool enough to be perfectly master of himself. This led him to say and do many wild and unaccountable things: By this, he said, he had broke the firm constitution of his health, that seemed so strong, that nothing was too hard for it; and he had suffered so much in his reputation, that he almost despaired to recover it. There were two principles in his natural temper that being heightened by that heat carried him to great excesses: a violent love of pleasure and a disposition to extravagant mirth. The one involved him in great sensuality: the other led him to many odd adventures and frolics, in which he was oft in hazard of his life. The one being the

41

same irregular appetite in his mind that the other was in his body, which made him think nothing diverting that was not extravagant. And though in cold blood he was a generous and good natured man, yet he would go far in his heats after anything that might turn to a jest or matter of diversion: He said to me he never improved his interest at Court to do a premeditate mischief to other persons. Yet he laid out his wit very freely in libels and satires, in which he had a peculiar talent of mixing his wit with his malice and fitting both with such apt words that men were tempted to be pleased with them: from thence his composures came to be easily known, for few had such a way of tempering those together as he had; so that when anything extraordinary that way came out, as a child is fathered sometimes by its resemblance, so it was laid at his door as its parent and author.

These exercises in the course of his life were not always equally pleasant to him; he had often sad intervals and severe reflections on them: and though then he had not these awakened in him from any deep principle of religion, yet the horror that Nature raised in him, especially in some sicknesses, made him too easy to receive some ill principles, which others endeavoured to possess him with; so that he was too soon brought to set himself too secure and fortify his mind against that, by dispossessing it all he could of the belief or apprehensions of religion. The licentiousness of his temper, with the briskness of his wit, disposed him to love the conversation of those who divided their time between lewd actions and irregular mirth. And so he came to bend his wit and direct his studies and endeavours to support and strengthen these ill principles both in himself and others.

> Gilbert Burnet, *Some Passages of the Life and Death of the Right Honourable John Earl of Rochester*, London, 1680, pp. 11–15

'A Very Profane Wit'

(i)

. . . heard the silly discourse of the King, with his people about him, telling a story of my Lord Rochester's having his clothes stole, while he was with a wench; and his gold all gone, but his clothes found afterwards stuffed into a feather bed by the wench that stole them.

Samuel Pepys, Diary, 2 December 1668

(ii)

The King dining yesterday at the Dutch Ambassador's, after dinner they drank and were pretty merry; and among the rest of the King's company there was that worthy fellow my lord of Rochester, and Tom Killigrew, whose mirth and raillery offended the former so much that he did give Tom Killigrew a box on the ear in the King's presence, which do much give offence to the people here at Court, to see how cheap the King makes himself and the more, for that the King hath not only passed by the thing, and pardoned it to Rochester already, but this very morning the King did publicly walk up and down, and Rochester I saw with him as free as ever, to the King's everlasting shame, to have so idle a rogue his companion. How Tom Killigrew takes it, I do not hear.

Samuel Pepys, Diary, 17 February 1668/9

(iii)

I dined with the Treasurer, where was the Earl of Rochester, a very profane wit.

John Evelyn, Diary, 24 November 1670

A Fiasco

[Perceptive readers will not need to be told that this account of a challenge in late November 1669 is coloured by malice. Mulgrave, third-rate poet and first-rate prig, was Rochester's inveterate enemy.]

During this time and heat of temper I had the good fortune not to be engaged in more than one quarrel; but that had somewhat in it singular enough to be related. I was informed that the Earl of

Rochester had said something of me which, according to his custom, was very malicious; I therefore sent Colonel Aston, a very mettled friend of mine, to call him to account for it. He denied the words, and indeed I was soon convinced that he had never said them; but the mere report, though I found it to be false, obliged me (as I then foolishly thought) to go on with the quarrel; and the next day was appointed for us to fight on horseback, a way in England a little unusual, but it was his part to choose. Accordingly, I and my second lay the night before at Knightsbridge privately, to avoid the being secured at London upon any suspicion; which yet we found ourselves more in danger of there, because we had all the appearance of highwaymen that had a mind to lie skulking in an odd inn for one night; but this I suppose the people of that house were used to, and so took no notice of us, but liked us the better. In the morning we met the Lord Rochester at the place appointed, who, instead of James Porter, whom he had assured Aston he would make his second, brought an errant lifeguardman whom nobody knew. To this Mr Aston took exception, upon the account of his being no suitable adversary; especially considering how extremely well he was mounted, whereas we had only a couple of pads: Upon which we all agreed to fight on foot. But as my Lord Rochester and I were riding into the next field in order to it, he told me that he had at first chosen to fight on horseback because he was so weak with a certain distemper, that he found himself unfit to fight at all any way, much less afoot. I was extremely surprised, because at that time no man had a better reputation for courage; and (my anger against him being quite over, because I was satisfied that he never spoke those words I resented) I took the liberty of representing what a ridiculous story it would make if we returned without fighting; and therefore advised him for both our sakes, especially for his own, to consider better of it; since I must be obliged in my own defence to lay the fault on him by telling the truth of the matter. His answer was, that he submitted to it and hoped that I would not desire the advantage of having to do with any man in so weak a condition. I replied that by such an argument he had sufficiently tied my hands, upon condition I might call our seconds to be witnesses of the whole business; which he consented to, and so we parted. When we returned to London, we found it full of this quarrel, upon our being absent so long; and therefore Mr Aston thought himself obliged to write down every word and circumstance of the whole matter, in order to spread everywhere the true reason of our returning without having fought; which, being never in the least either contradicted or resented by the Lord Rochester, entirely ruined his reputation as to courage (of which I was really sorry to be the occasion) though nobody had still a greater as to wit; which supported him pretty well in the world notwithstanding some more accidents of the same kind, that never fail to succeed one another when once people know a man's weakness.

> *Memoirs of His Grace John Duke of Buckingham, written by himself (Works of John Sheffield, Earl of Mulgrave, Marquis of Normanby and Duke of Buckingham,* II, London, 1723, pp. 8–10)

The Ballers

(i)

And so to supper in an arbour: but, Lord! their mad bawdy talk did make my heart ache! And here I first understood by their talk the meaning of the company that lately were called Ballers: Harris telling how it was by a meeting of some young blades, where he was among them, and my Lady Bennet and her ladies; and their there dancing naked, and all the roguish things of the world. But, Lord! what loose, cursed company was this, that I was in tonight, though full of wit; and worth a man's being in for once, to know the nature of it, and their manner of talk, and lives.

Samuel Pepys, *Diary*, 30 May 1668

(ii)

These
to the Rt. Honble.
the Earl of Rochester
humbly present

LONDON. Jan: the 26th. [1670/71]
My Lord of Rochester has so much obliged me by two letters of

different styles that I know not whether I ought to applaud most his good parts or his good nature, I am sure they neither of them need anything that I can say of them; in his Lps last letter my brother thinks himself as much concerned as I & therefore does join with me in most humble thanks. As to the former, my most deplorable excuse was made why I was not at the christening of my Ld. Wilmot by my Ld. Buckhurst & Sedley, it is a ceremony I was sorry to miss but yr. Lp. staying much with yr. Lady will I presume once a year furnish us with such solemnities, & for the next I hope I shall have no reason to fail paying my attendance, – in the meantime yr. Lp. has been extremely wanting here to make friends at the custom house where has been lately unfortunately seized a box of those leather instruments yr. Lp. carried down one of, but these barbarian farmers prompted by the villainous instigation of their wives voted them prohibited goods so that they were burnt without mercy notwithstanding that Sedley & I made two journeys into the City in their defence, – by this, my Ld., you see what things are done in yr. absence, & then pray consider whether it is fit for you to be blowing of coals in the country when there is a revenge due to the ashes of these martyrs, yr. Lp. is chosen general in this war betwixt the Ballers & the farmers, nor shall peace by my consent ever be made till they grant us our wine and our D's custom free. My Ld. Vaughan is come to town & has brought out of Wales several new arguments concerning some points you wot of, in fine here are so many reasons for yr. Lps. return hither that I know not how you can stay a moment where you are without breach of justice to your profession and of kindness to yr. friends who linger in your absence though they can not properly be said to thirst after you, being perpetually drinking yr. health, no man oftener nor in greater glasses than my Ld. of Rochester's most everything he would have me,

Hen. S. [i.e. Henry Savile]
British Museum, Harleian MS. 7003

From *Sodom*

[The play must have been composed no earlier than December 1670, since, as Pat Kearney has pointed out to me, its opening couplet parodies the first couplet of *The Conquest of Granada*.]

Act One

The scene an antichamber hung with Aretine's Postures.

[*Enter* BOLLOXIMIAN (*King of Sodom*), BORASTUS (*Bugger-master-General*), POCKANELLO (*pimp and favourite*), PINE *and* TULEY (*two pimps of honour*).]

BOLLOXIMIAN: Thus in the zenith of my lust I reign;
 I eat to swive and swive to eat again.
 Let other monarchs who their sceptres bear
 To keep their subjects less in love than fear
 Be slaves to crowns; my nation shall be free.
 My pintle only shall my sceptre be,
 My laws shall act more pleasure than command
 And with my prick I'll govern all the land.

POCKANELLO: Your Grace at once has from the powers above
 A knightly wisdom and a princely love
 Who doth permit your nation to enjoy
 That freedom which a tyrant would destroy.
 By this your royal tarse will purchase more
 Than all the riches of the kings of Zoar.

BORASTUS: May your most gracious prick and cods be still
 As boundless in their pleasure as your will,
 May plentiful delights of cunt and arse
 Be never wanting to your royal tarse,
 May lust endue your prick with flame and spright
 Ever to fuck with safety and delight.

BOLLOXIMIAN: My Lord Borastus, your judgment and your care
 Is now required in a nice affair.

BORASTUS: My duty's still my service to prepare.

BOLLOXIMIAN: You are our council all –

BORASTUS: The bliss we own.

BOLLOXIMIAN: But this advice belongs to you alone.
 Borastus! I no longer cunt admire;
 The drudgery has worn out my desire.

BORASTUS: Your Grace may soon to human arse retire.

Rouse, stately tarse, and let thy ballox grind;
Heave up, fair arse, and let my cunt be kind;
      Thrust pintle with a force
      Strong as any horse,
Spend till my cunt o'erflow,
Joined with the neighbouring flood of sperm below,
      When in a sound
      We lie as drowned
And dead upon the shore
Rather than wake or our sad leaves take,
   'Cause we can spend no more.

CHORUS: When pintles cannot give new breath
       The Resurrection's worse than Death.

Act Three

[Enter Prince PRICKETT *and Princess* SWIVEA.*]*

SWIVEA: Twelve months will pass ere that thou canst arrive
   To be a perfect man; that is, to swive
   As Pockanello –
   Your years to fifteen does but now incline.
PRICKETT: You know I would have stocked my prick at nine.
SWIVEA: I ne'er saw 't since; let's see how much 'tis grown.
   By heavens, a neat one. Now we're all alone
   I'll shut the door and you shall see my thing.
PRICKETT: Strange how it looks, methinks it smells like ling.
   It has a beard so sad! the mouth's all raw,
   The strangest creature that I ever saw –
   Are these the beasts that keep men in such awe?
SWIVEA: By such a thing philosophers have taught
   That all mankind into the world was brought.
   'Twas such a thing our sire, the King, bestrid,
   Out of whose loins we came –

PRICKETT: – The devil we did.
SWIVEA: It is the workhouse of the world's great trade;
    On this soft anvil all mankind was made.
    Come, 'tis a harmless thing. Draw near and try.
    You will desire no other death to die.
PRICKETT: Is't death then –
SWIVEA: – Ah, but with such pleasant pain
    That straight it tickles you to life again.
PRICKETT: I feel my spirits in an agony.
SWIVEA: These are the symptoms of young lechery.
    Does not your prick stand and your pulse beat fast?
    Don't you desire some unknown bliss to taste?
PRICKETT: My heart invites me to some new desire.
    My blood boils o'er –
SWIVEA: I can allay that fire.
    Come, my dear rogue, and on my belly lie.
    A little lower yet . . . now, dearest, try.
PRICKETT: I am a stranger to these unknown parts
    And never versed in Love's obliging arts.
    Pray guide me, I ne'er was this way before.
SWIVEA: Then enter now, since you have found the door.
PRICKETT: I'm in. I vow it is as soft as wool.
SWIVEA: Then thrust and move it up and down, you fool.

Act Four

[*Enter* BUGGERANTHUS (*General of the Army*).]

BORASTUS: My liege, the General.
BOLLOXIMIAN: – Brave man of war,
    How fares the Camp –
BUGGERANTHUS: Great sir, the soldiers are
    In double duties to your favours bound.
    They own it all, they swear and tear the ground,
    Protest they'll die with drinking of your health
    And creep into the other world by stealth,
    Intending there among the Gods to vye
    Our Sodom's King to immortality.
BOLLOXIMIAN: How are they pleased with what I did proclaim?

49

BUGGERANTHUS: They practise it in honour of your name.
  If lust present they want no woman's aid;
  Each buggers with consent his own comrade.
BOLLOXIMIAN: Besides, 'tis chargeable with cunts to play.
BUGGERANTHUS: This saves them, sir, at least a fortnight's pay –
  Then they do fuck and bugger one another
  And live like man and wife, sister and brother.
  Dildos and dogs with women do prevail;
  I caught one frigging with a cur's bob tail.
  'My Lord,' said she, 'I do it with remorse,
  For once I had a passion for a horse,
  Who in a moment grieved and pleased my heart.
  I saw him standing pensive in a cart,
  Whose padded eyes and back was sore oppressed,
  A heavy halter hanging on his crest.
  Grieved for the poor beast I stroked his mane,
  Pitied his daily labour and his pain,
  When on a sudden from his scabbard flew
  The stateliest yard that ever mortal drew,
  Which clinging to his belly stiff did stand.
  I took and grasped it in my loving hand
  And in a passion moved it to my cunt;
  But he, to womankind not being wont,
  Drew back his engine, though my cunt would spare
  Perhaps as much room as his lady mare.
  At length I found his constancy was such
  That he would none but his dear mistress touch.
  Urged by his scorn I from his sight depart
  And in despair surrender up my heart.
  Now wandering o'er this vile, cunt-starving land
  I am content with what comes next to hand.'
BOLLOXIMIAN: Such women ought to live. Pray find her out.
  She shall a pintle have both stiff and stout;
  Ballox shall hourly by her cunt be sucked,
  She shall be daily by all nations fucked.
  Industrious cunts should never pintle want;
  She shall be mistress to the Elephant.

British Museum, Harleian MS. 7312

50

'Odd Shapes'

He took pleasure to disguise himself as a porter or as a beggar; sometimes to follow some mean amours, which, for the variety of them, he affected; at other times merely for diversion, he would go about in odd shapes, in which he acted his part so naturally that even those who were on the secret and saw him in these shapes could perceive nothing by which he might be discovered.

> Gilbert Burnet, *Some Passages of the Life and Death of the Right Honourable John Earl of Rochester*, London, 1680, pp. 27, 28

Poems *c*. 1665–71

Song

'Twas a dispute 'twixt heaven and earth
Which had produced the nobler birth.
For heaven appeared Cynthia, with all her train,
    Till you came forth,
    More glorious and more worth
Than she with all those trembling imps of light
    With which this envious queen of night
Had proudly decked her conquered self in vain.

I must have perished in that first surprise,
    Had I beheld your eyes.
Love, like Apollo when he would inspire
Some holy breast, laid all his glories by;
Else the god, clothed in his heavenly fire,
    Would have possessed too powerfully
And, making of his priest a sacrifice,
Had so returned unhallowed to the skies.

A Dialogue between Strephon and Daphne

STREPHON
Prithee now, fond fool, give o'er.
Since my heart is gone before,

51

To what purpose should I stay?
Love commands another way.

DAPHNE

Perjured swain, I knew the time
When dissembling was your crime;
In pity now employ that art
Which first betrayed, to ease my heart.

STREPHON

Women can with pleasure feign;
Men dissemble still with pain.
What advantage will it prove
If I lie, who cannot love?

DAPHNE

Tell me, then, the reason why
Love from hearts in love does fly,
Why the bird will build a nest
Where he ne'er intends to rest?

STREPHON

Love, like other little boys,
Cries for hearts, as they for toys
Which, when gained, in childish play
Wantonly are thrown away.

DAPHNE

Still on wing, or on his knees,
Love does nothing by degrees:
Basely flying when most prized,
Meanly fawning when despised,
Flattering or insulting ever,
Generous and grateful never.
All his joys are fleeting dreams,
All his woes severe extremes.

STREPHON

Nymph, unjustly you inveigh:
Love, like us, must fate obey.
Since 'tis nature's law to change,
Constancy alone is strange.
See the heavens in lightnings break,
Next in storms of thunder speak,
Till a kind rain from above
Makes a calm — so 'tis in love.
Flames begin our first address;
Like meeting thunder we embrace;
Then, you know, the showers that fall
Quench the fire and quiet all.

DAPHNE

How should I these showers forget?
'Twas so pleasant to be wet!
They killed love, I knew it well:
I died all the while they fell.
Say, at least, what nymph it is
Robs my breast of so much bliss!
If she's fair, I shall be eased;
Through my ruin you'll be pleased.

STREPHON

Daphne never was so fair,
Strephon scarcely so sincere;
Gentle, innocent, and free,
Ever pleased with only me.
Many charms my heart enthrall,
But there's one above them all:
With aversion she does fly
Tedious, trading constancy.

DAPHNE

Cruel shepherd, I submit:
Do what love and you think fit.
Change is fate, and not design;
Say you would have still been mine.

STREPHON

Nymph, I cannot; 'tis too true,
Change has greater charms than you.
Be by my example wise:
Faith to pleasure sacrifice.

DAPHNE

Silly swain, I'll have you know
'Twas my practice long ago.
Whilst you vainly thought me true,
I was false in scorn of you.
By my tears, my heart's disguise,
I thy love and thee despise.
Womankind more joy discovers
Making fools, than keeping lovers.

The Platonic Lady

I could love thee till I die,
Wouldst thou love me modestly,
And ne'er press, whilst I live,
For more than willingly I would give:
   Which should sufficient be to prove
   I'd understand the art of love.

I hate the thing is called enjoyment.
Besides, it is a dull employment;
It cuts off all that's life and fire
From that which may be termed desire,
   Just like the bee whose sting is gone
   Converts its owner to a drone.

I love a youth will give me leave
His body in my arms to wreathe,
To press him gently and to kiss,

To sigh and look with eyes that wish
  For what, if I could once obtain,
  I would neglect with flat disdain.

I'd give him liberty to toy
And play with me, and count it joy.
Our freedom should be full complete,
And nothing wanting but the feat.
  Let's practise, then, and we shall prove
  These are the only sweets of love.

Song

As Chloris full of harmless thought
Beneath the willows lay,
Kind love a comely shepherd brought
To pass the time away.

She blushed to be encountered so
And chid the amorous swain,
But as she strove to rise and go,
He pulled her back again.

A sudden passion seized her heart
In spite of her disdain;
She found a pulse in every part
And love in every vein.

'Ah, youth!' quoth she. 'What charms are these
That conquer and surprise?
Ah, let me – for unless you please,
I have no power to rise.'

She faintly spoke, and trembling lay,
For fear he should comply,
But virgins' eyes their hearts betray
And give their tongues the lie.

Thus she, who princes had denied
With all their pompous train,
Was in the lucky minute tried
And yielded to the swain.

Song

Fair Chloris in a pigsty lay;
Her tender herd lay by her.
She slept; in murmuring gruntlings they,
Complaining of the scorching day,
Her slumbers thus inspire.

She dreamt whilst she with careful pains
Her snowy arms employed
In ivory pails to fill out grains,
One of her love-convicted swains
Thus hasting to her cried:

'Fly, nymph! Oh, fly ere 'tis too late
A dear, loved life to save;
Rescue your bosom pig from fate
Who now expires, hung in the gate
That leads to Flora's cave.

'Myself had tried to set him free
Rather than brought the news,
But I am so abhorred by thee
That ev'n thy darling's life from me
I know thou wouldst refuse.'

Struck with the news, as quick she flies
As blushes to her face;
Not the bright lightning from the skies,
Nor love, shot from her brighter eyes,
Move half so swift a pace.

This plot, it seems, the lustful slave
Had laid against her honour,
Which not one god took care to save,
For he pursues her to the cave
And throws himself upon her.

Now piercèd is her virgin zone;
She feels the foe within it.
She hears a broken amorous groan,
The panting lover's fainting moan,
Just in the happy minute.

Frighted she wakes, and waking frigs.
Nature thus kindly eased
In dreams raised by her murmuring pigs
And her own thumb between her legs,
She's innocent and pleased.

3

'The Imperfect Enjoyment'

1672	*17 March*. Third Dutch War began. Rochester took no part in it.
	Late spring and summer at his wife's estate at Enmore, Somerset, and his own at Adderbury, Oxfordshire.
	31 October. Appointed Deputy Lieutenant of Somerset.
1673	Love-affair with Elizabeth Barry began.

Two Stories from Adderbury

[These tales, passed from generation to generation, were still being told by the villagers of Adderbury at the end of the First World War. They were collected by H. J. Gepp and published in his *Adderbury* (Banbury, 1924). V. de Sola Pinto, in his standard biography of Rochester, has drawn on Gepp, but carelessly, setting the first story not at Barford, to the south-west of Adderbury, but at Burford, where Rochester went to school.]

He went to Barford disguised as a tinker and asked the people for their pots and pans to mend. On receiving them he knocked the bottoms out, whereupon he was put in the stocks. He then persuaded a man to take a note from him to Lord Rochester at Adderbury, upon which his carriage and four arrived at Barford, the stocks were dug up and he returned home. Shortly afterwards he sent the people new pots and pans. On another occasion he disguised himself as a tramp and on meeting a tramp he asked him where he was going. The latter replied that he was going to Lord Rochester's, not that it was of any use, for he never gave anything. Lord Rochester said he would go with him. The tramp went to the back of the house, while Lord Rochester went to the front and gave the servants instructions to detain him and put him in a barrel of beer. Every time the tramp put his head up the Earl threatened to 'bash him' and he kept him there for some time. On releasing him he gave him a good meal and a new suit of clothes, and told him never again to say there was nothing to be got from Lord Rochester.

Adderbury, p. 59

The Felicity of Last Summer

[This letter, 'For the right hon^ble the Earl of Rochester at the Arbor house in Portugal row in Lincolns Inn fields', was written by Henry Bulkeley, later the King's Master of the Household, probably some time in March 1672, since his company of foot landed at Chester on 2 April. Its mention of the Bear and 'talk of nothing but fighting & fucking' recalls the opening lines of 'A Ramble in St James's Park'.]

My dear Lord,

Though there is no man living more faithfully concerned than I am at any good or ill that can happen to you, yet I don't wonder you fall into such persecutions as the last, since you live in an age when fools are the most powerful enemies & the few wise we have either cannot or will not befriend us, since the fop is the only fine gentleman of the times & a committee of those able statesmen assemble daily to talk of nothing but fighting & fucking at Lockett's & will never be reconciled to men who speak sense & reason at the Bear or Covent Garden. It is they are the hopeful sprigs of the Nation whose knowledge lies in their light periwigs & trimmed shoes, who herd with one another not because they love themselves but understand nobody else, whose honour, honesty & friendship is like the consent of hounds, who know not why they run together but that they hunt the same scent, fellows that would make the world believe that they are not afraid of dying & yet are out of heart if the wind disorders their hair or ruffles their cravats. . . .

I hope it won't now be long before I shall be so happy as to wait upon your Lordship, for I have received the King's commands to march with my company to London. In order to it I shall, I believe, embark within a fortnight for Chester & so on, where if I may live in the same felicity I enjoyed last summer in the honour of being near you, I have my greatest aim, for I am, with all the unreservedness in the world,

> My Lord
> Your most faithful humble servant
> H. Bulkeley.

British Museum, Harleian MS. 7003

Friendship with Dryden

(i)

That which with more reason I admire is that, being so absolute a courtier, you have not forgot either the ties of friendship or the practice of generosity. In my little experience of a Court (which I confess I desire not to improve) I have found in it much of interest and more of detraction: Few men there have that assurance of a friend as not to be made ridiculous by him when they are absent.

> John Dryden, *Marriage-à-la Mode*, 1672; dedication 'To the Right Honourable the Earl of Rochester'

(ii)

You see, my Lord, how far you have pushed me; I dare not own the honour you have done me, for fear of showing it to my own disadvantage. You are that Rerum Natura of your own Lucretius, Ipsa suis pollens opibus, nihil indiga nostri: You are above any incense I can give you; and have all the happiness of an idle life, joined with the good nature of an active. Your friends in town are ready to envy the leisure you have given yourself in the country: though they know you are only their steward and that you treasure up but so much health as you intend to spend on them in winter.

> John Dryden, letter of July(?) 1673, British Museum, Harleian MS. 7003

[Elizabeth Barry was a girl Rochester trained as an actress. He persevered with her even after a humiliating failure, and she lived to become 'the famous Mrs Barry', described by Dryden as 'always excellent'.

Letters from Rochester to her were preserved, and it is natural to associate with her the song, 'Leave this gaudy, gilded stage,' in the autograph manuscript at Nottingham.]

(i)

Song

Leave this gaudy, gilded stage,
From custom more than use frequented,
Where fools of either sex and age
Crowd to see themselves presented.
To Love's theatre, the bed,
Youth and Beauty fly together,
And act so well it may be said
The laurel there was due to either.
'Twixt strife of Love and war the difference lies in this:
When neither overcomes, Love's triumph greater is.

(ii)

MADAM,

So much wit and beauty as you have should think of nothing less than doing miracles; and there cannot be a greater than to continue to love me: affecting everything is mean, as loving pleasure, and being fond where you find merit; but to pick out the wildest and most fantastical odd man alive, and to place your kindness there, is an act so brave and daring as will show the greatness of your spirit, and distinguish you in love, as you are in all things else, from womankind. Whether I have made a good argument for myself, I leave you to judge; and beg you to believe me, whenever I tell you what Mrs R. is, since I give you so sincere an account of her humblest servant: Remember the hour of a strict account, when both hearts are to be open, and we obliged to speak freely, as you ordered it yesterday, for so I must ever call the day I saw you last, since all time between that and the next visit is no part of my life, or at least like a long fit of the falling-sickness, wherein I am dead to all joy and happiness. Here's a damned impertinent fool bolted in, that hinders me from ending my letter; the plague of — take him, and any man or woman alive that takes my thoughts off of you: But in the evening I will see you and be happy in spite of all the fools in the world.

Dear MADAM,

You are stark mad, and therefore the fitter for me to love; and that is the reason, I think, I can never leave to be
Your humble servant

Familiar Letters: Written by the Right Honourable John late Earl of Rochester and Several other Persons of Honour and Quality (ed. Charles Gildon) II, London, 1697, pp. 1, 2, 7

Poems *c.* 1672–3

Two Translations from Lucretius

I

Great Mother of Aeneas, and of Love;
Delight of mankind, and the powers above;
Who all beneath those sprinkled drops of light
Which slide upon the face of gloomy night,
Whither vast regions of that liquid world
Where groves of ships on watery hills are hurled,
Or fruitful earth, dost bless, since 'tis by thee
That all things live which the bright sun does see. . . .

II

The gods, by right of nature, must possess
An everlasting age of perfect peace,
Far off removed from us and our affairs,
Neither approached by dangers or by cares,
Rich in themselves, to whom we cannot add,
Not pleased by good deeds, nor provoked by bad.

To Love
(from Ovid's *Amores*)

O Love! how cold and slow to take my part,
Thou idle wanderer about my heart.
Why thy old faithful soldier wilt thou see
Oppressed in my own tents? They murder me.
Thy flames consume, thy arrows pierce thy friends;
Rather, on foes pursue more noble ends.
    Achilles' sword would generously bestow
A cure as certain as it gave the blow.
Hunters who follow flying game give o'er
When the prey's caught; hope still leads on before.
We thine own slaves feel thy tyrannic blows,
Whilst thy tame hand's unmoved against thy foes.
On men disarmed how can you gallant prove?
And I was long ago disarmed by love.
Millions of dull men live, and scornful maids:
We'll own Love valiant when he these invades.
Rome from each corner of the wide world snatched
A laurel; else 't had been to this day thatched.
    But the old soldier has his resting place,
And the good battered horse is turned to grass.
The harassed whore, who lived a wretch to please,
Has leave to be a bawd and take her ease.
For me, then, who have freely spent my blood,
Love, in thy service, and so boldly stood
In Celia's trenches, were 't not wisely done
E'en to retire, and live at peace at home?

No! Might I gain a godhead to disclaim

My glorious title to my endless flame,
Divinity with scorn I would forswear,
Such sweet, dear, tempting mischiefs women are.
Whene'er those flames grow faint, I quickly find
A fierce black storm pour down upon my mind.
Headlong I'm hurled, like horsemen who in vain
Their fury-foaming coursers would restrain.
As ships, just when the harbour they attain,
By sudden blasts are snatched to sea again,
So Love's fantastic storms reduce my heart
Half-rescued, and the god resumes his dart.

Strike here, this undefended bosom wound,
And for so brave a conquest be renowned.
Shafts fly so fast to me from every part,
You'll scarce discern your quiver from my heart.
What wretch can bear a livelong night's dull rest,
Or think himself in lazy slumbers blessed?
Fool! Is not sleep the image of pale death?
There's time for rest when fate has stopped your breath.
Me may my soft deluding dear deceive:
I'm happy in my hopes whilst I believe.
Now let her flatter, then as fondly chide:
Often may I enjoy, oft be denied.

With doubtful steps the god of war does move
By thy example led, ambiguous Love.
Blown to and fro like down from thy own wing,
Who knows when joy or anguish thou wilt bring?
Yet at thy mother's and thy slave's request,
Fix an eternal empire in my breast;
  And let th' inconstant charming sex,
  Whose wilful scorn does lovers vex,
  Submit their hearts before thy throne:
  The vassal world is then thy own.

The Imperfect Enjoyment

Naked she lay, clasped in my longing arms,
I filled with love, and she all over charms;

Both equally inspired with eager fire,
Melting through kindness, flaming in desire.
With arms, legs, lips close clinging to embrace,
She clips me to her breast, and sucks me to her face.
Her nimble tongue, Love's lesser lightning, played
Within my mouth, and to my thoughts conveyed
Swift orders that I should prepare to throw
The all-dissolving thunderbolt below.
My fluttering soul, sprung with the pointed kiss,
Hangs hovering o'er her balmy brinks of bliss.
But whilst her busy hand would guide that part
Which should convey my soul up to her heart,
In liquid raptures I dissolve all o'er,
Melt into sperm, and spend at every pore.
A touch from any part of her had done 't:
Her hand, her foot, her very look's a cunt.

  Smiling, she chides in a kind murmuring noise,
And from her body wipes the clammy joys,
When, with a thousand kisses wandering o'er
My panting bosom, 'Is there then no more?'
She cries. 'All this to love and rapture's due;
Must we not pay a debt to pleasure too?'

  But I, the most forlorn, lost man alive,
To show my wished obedience vainly strive:
I sigh, alas! and kiss, but cannot swive.
Eager desires confound my first intent,
Succeeding shame does more success prevent,
And rage at last confirms me impotent.
Ev'n her fair hand, which might bid heat return
To frozen age, and make cold hermits burn,
Applied to my dead cinder, warms no more
Than fire to ashes could past flames restore.
Trembling, confused, despairing, limber, dry,
A wishing, weak, unmoving lump I lie.
This dart of love, whose piercing point, oft tried,
With virgin blood ten thousand maids have dyed;
Which nature still directed with such art
That it through every cunt reached every heart —

Stiffly resolved, 'twould carelessly invade
Woman or man, nor ought its fury stayed:
Where'er it pierced, a cunt it found or made –
Now languid lies in this unhappy hour,
Shrunk up and sapless like a withered flower.

Thou treacherous, base deserter of my flame,
False to my passion, fatal to my fame,
Through what mistaken magic dost thou prove
So true to lewdness, so untrue to love?
What oyster-cinder-beggar-common whore
Didst thou e'er fail in all thy life before?
When vice, disease, and scandal lead the way,
With what officious haste dost thou obey!
Like a rude, roaring hector in the streets
Who scuffles, cuffs, and justles all he meets,
But if his King or country claim his aid,
The rakehell villain shrinks and hides his head;
Ev'n so thy brutal valour is displayed,
Breaks every stew, does each small whore invade,
But when great Love the onset does command,
Base recreant to thy prince, thou dar'st not stand.
Worst part of me, and henceforth hated most,
Through all the town a common fucking post,
On whom each whore relieves her tingling cunt
As hogs on gates do rub themselves and grunt,
Mayst thou to ravenous chancres be a prey,
Or in consuming weepings waste away;
May strangury and stone thy days attend;
May'st thou ne'er piss, who didst refuse to spend
When all my joys did on false thee depend.

And may ten thousand abler pricks agree
To do the wronged Corinna right for thee.

A Ramble in St James's Park

Much wine had passed, with grave discourse
Of who fucks who, and who does worse
(Such as you usually do hear

From those that diet at the Bear),
When I, who still take care to see
Drunkenness relieved by lechery,
Went out into St James's Park
To cool my head and fire my heart.
But though St James has th' honour on 't,
'Tis consecrate to prick and cunt.
There, by a most incestuous birth,
Strange woods spring from the teeming earth;
For they relate how heretofore,
When ancient Pict began to whore,
Deluded of his assignation
(Jilting, it seems, was then in fashion),
Poor pensive lover, in this place
Would frig upon his mother's face;
Whence rows of mandrakes tall did rise
Whose lewd tops fucked the very skies.
Each imitative branch does twine
In some loved fold of Aretine,
And nightly now beneath their shade
Are buggeries, rapes, and incests made.
Unto this all-sin-sheltering grove
Whores of the bulk and the alcove,
Great ladies, chambermaids, and drudges,
The ragpicker, and heiress trudges.
Carmen, divines, great lords, and tailors,
Prentices, poets, pimps, and jailers,
Footmen, fine fops do here arrive,
And here promiscuously they swive.
   Along these hallowed walks it was
That I beheld Corinna pass.
Whoever had been by to see
The proud disdain she cast on me
Through charming eyes, he would have swore
She dropped from heaven that very hour,
Forsaking the divine abode
In scorn of some despairing god.
But mark what creatures women are:

How infinitely vile, when fair!

Three knights o' th' elbow and the slur
With wriggling tails made up to her.

The first was of your Whitehall blades,
Near kin t' th' Mother of the Maids;
Graced by whose favour he was able
To bring a friend t' th' Waiters' table,
Where he had heard Sir Edward Sutton
Say how the King loved Banstead mutton;
Since when he'd ne'er be brought to eat
By 's good will any other meat.
In this, as well as all the rest,
He ventures to do like the best,
But wanting common sense, th' ingredient
In choosing well not least expedient,
Converts abortive imitation
To universal affectation.
Thus he not only eats and talks
But feels and smells, sits down and walks,
Nay looks, and lives, and loves by rote,
In an old tawdry birthday coat.

The second was a Grays Inn wit,
A great inhabiter of the pit,
Where critic-like he sits and squints,
Steals pocket handkerchiefs, and hints,
From 's neighbour, and the comedy,
To court, and pay, his landlady.

The third, a lady's eldest son
Within few years of twenty-one,
Who hopes from his propitious fate,
Against he comes to his estate,
By these two worthies to be made
A most accomplished tearing blade.

One, in a strain 'twixt tune and nonsense,
Cries, 'Madam, I have loved you long since.
Permit me your fair hand to kiss';
When at her mouth her cunt cries, 'Yes!'
In short, without much more ado,

Joyful and pleased, away she flew,
And with these three confounded asses
From park to hackney coach she passes.
    So a proud bitch does lead about
Of humble curs the amorous rout,
Who most obsequiously do hunt
The savoury scent of salt-swoln cunt.
Some power more patient now relate
The sense of this surprising fate.
Gods! that a thing admired by me
Should fall to so much infamy.
Had she picked out, to rub her arse on,
Some stiff-pricked clown or well-hung parson,
Each job of whose spermatic sluice
Had filled her cunt with wholesome juice,
I the proceeding should have praised
In hope sh' had quenched a fire I raised.
Such natural freedoms are but just:
There's something generous in mere lust.
But to turn damned abandoned jade
When neither head nor tail persuade;
To be a whore in understanding,
A passive pot for fools to spend in!
The devil played booty, sure, with thee
To bring a blot on infamy.
    But why am I, of all mankind,
To so severe a fate designed?
Ungrateful! Why this treachery
To humble, fond, believing me,
Who gave you privilege above
The nice allowances of love?
Did ever I refuse to bear
The meanest part your lust could spare?
When your lewd cunt came spewing home
Drenched with the seed of half the town,
My dram of sperm was supped up after
For the digestive surfeit water.
Full gorgèd at another time

With a vast meal of nasty slime
Which your devouring cunt had drawn
From porters' backs and footmen's brawn,
I was content to serve you up
My ballock-full for your grace cup,
Nor ever thought it an abuse
While you had pleasure for excuse –
You that could make my heart away
For noise and colour, and betray
The secrets of my tender hours
To such knight-errant paramours,
When, leaning on your faithless breast,
Wrapped in security and rest,
Soft kindness all my powers did move,
And reason lay dissolved in love!
     May stinking vapours choke your womb
Such as the men you dote upon!
May your depravèd appetite,
That could in whiffling fools delight,
Beget such frenzies in your mind
You may go mad for the north wind,
And fixing all your hopes upon 't
To have him bluster in your cunt,
Turn up your longing arse t' th' air
And perish in a wild despair!
But cowards shall forget to rant,
Schoolboys to frig, old whores to paint;
The Jesuits' fraternity
Shall leave the use of buggery;
Crab-louse, inspired with grace divine,
From earthly cod to heaven shall climb;
Physicians shall believe in Jesus,
And disobedience cease to please us,
Ere I desist with all my power
To plague this woman and undo her.
But my revenge will best be timed
When she is married that is limed.
In that most lamentable state

I'll make her feel my scorn and hate:
Pelt her with scandals, truth or lies,
And her poor cur with jealousies,
Till I have torn him from her breech,
While she whines like a dog-drawn bitch;
Loathed and despised, kicked out o' th' Town
Into some dirty hole alone,
To chew the cud of misery
And know she owes it all to me.
   And may no woman better thrive
   That dares profane the cunt I swive!

The Second Prologue at Court to *The Empress of Morocco*, Spoken by the Lady Elizabeth Howard

Wit has of late took up a trick t' appear
Unmannerly, or at the best severe,
And poets share the fate by which we fall
When kindly we attempt to please you all.
'Tis hard your scorn should against such prevail
Whose ends are to divert you, though they fail.
You men would think it an ill-natured jest
Should we laugh at you when you did your best.
Then rail not here, though you see reason for 't:
If wit can find itself no better sport,
Wit is a very foolish thing at Court.
Wit's business is to please, and not to fright:
'Tis no wit to be always in the right;
You'll find it none, who dare be so tonight.
Few so ill-bred will venture to a play
To spy out faults in what we women say.
For us, no matter *what* we speak, but *how*:
How kindly can we say, 'I hate you now!'
And for the men, if you'll laugh at 'em, do:
They mind themselves so much, they'll ne'er mind you.
   But why do I descend to lose a prayer
On those small saints in wit? The god sits *there*.

[To the King]

To you, great sir, my message hither tends
From youth and beauty, your allies and friends.
See my credentials written in my face:
They challenge your protection in this place,
And hither come with such a force of charms
As may give check ev'n to your prosperous arms.
Millions of cupids, hovering in the rear,
Like eagles following fatal troops appear,
All waiting for the slaughter which draws nigh
Of those bold gazers who this night must die;
Nor can you 'scape our soft captivity,
From which old age alone must set you free.
Then tremble at the fatal consequence,
Since 'tis well known, for your own part, great prince,
'Gainst us you still have made a weak defence.
Be generous and wise, and take our part;
Remember we have eyes, and you a heart.
Else you may find, too late, that we are things
Born to kill vassals and to conquer kings.
    But, oh! to what vain conquest I pretend
Whilst Love is our commander, and your friend.
Our victory your empire more assures,
For Love will ever make the triumph yours.

Song

Love a woman? You're an ass!
'Tis a most insipid passion
To choose out for your happiness
The silliest part of God's creation.

Let the porter and the groom,
Things designed for dirty slaves,
Drudge in fair Aurelia's womb
To get supplies for age and graves.

Farewell, woman! I intend
Henceforth every night to sit
With my lewd, well-natured friend,
Drinking to engender wit.

Then give me health, wealth, mirth, and wine,
And, if busy love entrenches,
There's a sweet, soft page of mine
Does the trick worth forty wenches.

Grecian Kindness

The utmost grace the Greeks could show,
When to the Trojans they grew kind,
Was with their arms to let 'em go
And leave their lingering wives behind.
They beat the men, and burnt the town:
Then all the baggage was their own.

There the kind deity of wine
Kissed the soft wanton god of love;
This clapped his wings, that pressed his vine,
And their best powers united move;
While each brave Greek embraced his punk,
Lulled her asleep, and then grew drunk.

A Satire on Charles II

I' th' isle of Britain, long since famous grown
For breeding the best cunts in Christendom,
There reigns, and oh! long may he reign and thrive,
The easiest King and best-bred man alive.
Him no ambition moves to get renown
Like the French fool, that wanders up and down
Starving his people, hazarding his crown.
Peace is his aim, his gentleness is such,

And love he loves, for he loves fucking much.
  Nor are his high desires above his strength:
His sceptre and his prick are of a length;
And she may sway the one who plays with th'other,
And make him little wiser than his brother.
Poor prince! thy prick, like thy buffoons at Court,
Will govern thee because it makes thee sport.
'Tis sure the sauciest prick that e'er did swive,
The proudest, peremptoriest prick alive.
Though safety, law, religion, life lay on 't,
'Twould break through all to make its way to cunt.
Restless he rolls about from whore to whore,
A merry monarch, scandalous and poor.

  To Carwell, the most dear of all his dears,
The best relief of his declining years,
Oft he bewails his fortune, and her fate:
To love so well, and be beloved so late.
For though in her he settles well his tarse,
Yet his dull, graceless ballocks hang an arse.
This you'd believe, had I but time to tell ye
The pains it costs to poor, laborious Nelly,
Whilst she employs hands, fingers, mouth and thighs,
Ere she can raise the member she enjoys.

  All monarchs I hate, and the thrones they sit on,
  From the hector of France to the cully of Britain.

4

'The Right Vein'

1673/4	*27 February*. Rochester made Ranger of Woodstock Park. This entitled him to use the High Lodge.
	2 May. Became Keeper of Woodstock Park.
	13 July. Baptism of Elizabeth, his third child.
1675	*25 June*. Drunk, he smashed the dials in the Privy Garden at Whitehall.

In Woodstock Park

(i)

His youthly spirit and opulent fortune did sometimes make him do extravagant actions, but in the country he was generally civil enough. He was wont to say that when he came to Brentford the Devil entered into him and never left him till he came into the country again, to Alderbury or Woodstock.

He was ranger of Woodstock Park and lived often at the lodge at the west end, a very delightful place and noble prospect westwards. Here his lordship had several lascivious pictures drawn.

John Aubrey, *Brief Lives*

(ii)

This Lord (who died at the High Lodge in Woodstock, July 26, 1680) used sometimes, with others of his companions, to run naked, and particularly they did so once in Woodstock Park, upon a Sunday in the afternoon, expecting that several of the female sex would have been spectators, but not one appeared. The man that stripped them, & pulled off their shirts, kept the shirts, & did not deliver them any more, going off with them before they finished the race. . . . Once the wild Earl of Rochester and some of his companions, a little way from Woodstock, meeting in a morning with a fine young maid going with butter to market, they bought all the butter of her, and paid her for it, & afterwards stuck it up against a tree, which the maid perceiving after they were gone, she went & took it off, thinking it pity that it should be quite spoiled. They observed her, &, riding after her, soon overtook her &, as a punishment, set her upon her head & clapped the butter upon her breech. . . .

The said Earl of Rochester . . . (among other girls) used the body of one Nell Browne of Woodstock, who, though she looked pretty well when clean, yet she was a very nasty, ordinary, silly creature, which made people much admire.

7 and 8 January 1725/6; Thomas Hearne, *Remarks and Collections*, IX, Oxford, 1914, pp. 78 and 79

(iii)

He would often go into the country and be for some months wholly employed in study or the sallies of his wit: which he came to direct chiefly to satire. And this he often defended to me, by saying there were some people that could not be kept in order or admonished but in this way.

Gilbert Burnet, *Some Passages of the Life and Death of the Right Honourable John Earl of Rochester*, London, 1680, p. 25

'The Right Vein'

His lordship read all manner of books. Mr Andrew Marvell, who was a good judge of wit, was wont to say that he was the best English satirist and had the right vein. 'Twas pity death took him off so soon.

John Aubrey, *Brief Lives*

All poems in their dedications ought to return to your Lordship, as all rivers to the sea, from whose depth and saltness they are seasoned and supplied: none of them ever coming to your Lordship's hands without receiving some of the rich tinctures of your unerring judgement; and running with much more clearness, having past so fine a strainer. If this receives any approbation in the world, I must ascribe it principally to your Lordship's partial recommendations and impartial corrections. . . . Judgement and fancy, seldom concurring in other men, in any small proportion, are possessed by your Lordship in the highest degree that ever was allowed in the soul of man; yet with so happy and harmonious a mixture that neither of them predominate nor usurp; but, like two peaceful colleagues in empire, agree within themselves and govern the rest of the world. . . . What was favourably said of my Lord Bacon in his time may much more justly be affirmed of your Lordship in yours; that if ever there were a beam of knowledge, immediately derived from God, upon any man, since the Creation, there is one upon yourself. Others, by wearisome steps and regular gradations, climb up to knowledge; your Lordship is flown up to the top of the hill: you are an enthusiast in wit; a poet and philosopher by revelation; and have already, in your tender age, set out such new and glorious lights in poetry, yet those so orthodox and unquestionable that all the heroes of Antiquity must submit or Homer and Virgil be judged Nonconformists. For my part, I account it one of the great felicities of my life to have lived in your age; but much greater to have had access to your person and to have been cherished and enlightened by the influences and irradiations of so great a luminary. For, I must confess, I never return from your Lordship's most charming and instructive conversation but I am inspired with a new genius and improved in all those sciences I ever coveted the knowledge of: I find myself not only a better poet, a better philosopher, but, much more than these, a better Christian: your Lordship's miraculous wit and intellectual powers being the greatest argument that ever I could meet with for the immateriality of the soul; they being the highest exaltation of humane nature; and, under Divine Authority, much more convincing to suspicious Reason than all the pedantic proofs of the most learnedly peevish disputants: so that, I hope, I shall be obliged to your Lordship not only for my reputation in this world but my future happiness in the next. Reflect then, my Lord, I beseech you, on your own sublime perfections, the profuseness of your favours, my powerful (though presumptuous) inclination to your person, and judge if it be possible for any other man living to pay your Lordship so sincere and affectionate a veneration as

My Lord,
Your Lordship's most devoted,
obedient and humble servant,
FRANCIS FANE

Sir Francis Fane, Dedicatory Epistle to *Love in the Dark*, London, 1675

The Smashing of the Phallic Dials

[Franciscus Linus] printed a discourse of dialling in 4to, Latin, and made the Jesuits' College there [in Liège] the finest dials in the world, which are described in that book. The like dials he made (which resemble something a . . . of candlesticks) in the garden at Whitehall, which were one night, anno Dni. 167– (4to, as I take it), broken all to pieces (for they were of glass spheres) by the Earl of Rochester, Lord Buckhurst, Fleetwood Shephard, etc. coming in from their revels. 'What!' said the Earl of Rochester, 'doest thou stand here to . . . Time?' Dash they set to work. There was a watchman always stood there to secure it.

John Aubrey, *Brief Lives*; (Life of Franciscus Linus)

The Alexander Bendo Episode

(i)

For his other studies, they were divided between the comical and witty writings of the Ancients and Moderns, the Roman authors, and books of physic: which the ill state of health he was fallen into made more necessary to himself: and which qualified him for an odd adventure, which I shall but just mention. Being under an unlucky accident, which obliged him to keep out of the way, he disguised himself, so that his nearest friends could not have known him, and set up in Tower Street for an Italian mountebank, where he had a stage and practised physic for some weeks, not without success.

Gilbert Burnet, *Some Passages of the Life and Death of the Right Honourable John Earl of Rochester*, London, 1680, pp. 26, 27

(ii)

[In 1687, as a New Year gift for Rochester's daughter Anne, Thomas Alcock, who had been Rochester's servant, wrote an account of the 'Italian mountebank'. The complete manuscript was edited in 1961 by V. de Sola Pinto under the title *The Famous Pathologist* (*Nottingham University Miscellany*, No. 1).]

And I wish it possible for me by this narrative to procure your Ladyship that real mirth and continual hearty laughs such news as this frequently gave us whilst we plyed our peculiar operations in the laboratory; some stirring an old boiling kettle, of soot and urine, tinged with a little asafetida and all the nasty ingredients that would render the smell more unsavoury, others tending the fires, some luting the retorts, others pounding bricks and scraping powders from them:

Here one busy calcining the minerals, there another scumming a crucible; some grinding oils, with a stone upon marble, till they sweat again; whilst the drops from face and nose made the medicine the bigger and consequently more beneficial; others labouring at the pestle & mortar, and all of them dressed like the old witches in Macbeth, whilst the grave and wise, the civil, modest and just pathologist, the noble Doctor Alexander Bendo, in an old over-grown green gown which he religiously wore in memory of Rabelais his master, put on at the reception of his Doctor's degree at Montpellier, lined through with exotic furs of diverse colours, an antique cap, a great reverend beard, and a magnificient false medal set round with glittering pearl, rubies, and diamonds of the same cognation, hung about his neck in a massy goldlike chain of princes' metal, which the King of Cyprus (you must know) had given him for doing a signal cure upon his darling daughter, the Princess Aloephangina, who was painted in a banner and hung up at his elbow, sat with his scales and weights, making up medicines of all sorts and sealing them with his seal of office, giving pretended directions to his operators by his indicative gestures in a language which neither he nor they understood one word of; for though we had Latin, French and Italian to use on occasion, yet since our mystery (as all trades else) flourished best under the deep recesses of concealment and secrecy, we of the fraternity kept a perpetual jangling to one another, as if we were mighty industrious and intent upon our respective operations, in a jargon of damned unintelligible gibberish all the while, & indeed we judged it not convenient, in our circumstances, to do anything in plain English but laugh.

And all this to amuse the gentle spectators, whom we freely admitted into our laboratory, that they might see we took pains for what we had and consequently were no cheats, as the arbitrarious apothecaries had endeavoured to represent us: But by this means alone we out-cheated them a bar and a half, which was a great part of our business and beneficial recreation.

But ah! fading joys! the pleasures we had so long fed on were now become meat for our masters and the hungry Court could no longer sustain her drooping spirits without the intellectual viands we had hitherto feasted on; and (woe to his operators and many dependants) the noble Doctor (with sorrow to his desponding enemies & joy to his triumphant friends) was now called home, who made the quickest voyage from France that ever man did, which was the talk and admiration of the whole town, for those that saw his ostracism cancelled this night at Whitehall did the very next see him there in splendour dancing at a ball in as great favour as ever: & nobody knew what was become of the mountebanks.

It was some time rumoured that they were an enchanted crew, raised and laid by necromancy: and who so apt to believe this story (think ye) as their credulous patients, which made the twice deluded fools who had furnished themselves with medicines, as they thought, against all accidents whatsoever, throw them now away for fear of witchcraft.

The apothecaries really believed that the Devil was run away with them, for it was not known who or what they were till a long time after. The poor carpenters that set up the stage were glad to take it for their pains, and the goldsmith had the utensils left in the laboratory for the rent of his house, and I daresay he never saw one of his tenants since to his knowledge, nor the noble Doctor his landlord:

And this is as much as I can remember, fit to be spoken, of this famous pathologist, Doctor Bendo.

Nottingham University MS. 1489

(iii)

[Tonson and Curll, in their editions of Rochester's poems, print slightly different versions of Alexander Bendo's Bill. Thomas Alcock's transcription may be read in V. de Sola Pinto's *The Famous Pathologist*.]

To All
Gentlemen, Ladies & others
whether of
City, Town or Country:
Alexander Bendo
wisheth all Health and
Prosperity.

Whereas this famous metropolis of England (and were the endeavours of its worthy inhabitants equal to their power, merit and virtue, I should not stick to denounce it, in a short time, the metropolis of the whole world:) whereas, I say, this city (as most great ones are) has ever been infested with a numerous company of such whose arrogant confidence, backing their ignorance, has enabled them to impose upon the people either premeditated cheats or at best the palpable, dull & empty mistakes of their self-deluded imaginations, in physic, chymical and Galenic, in astrology, physiogromy, palmistry, mathematics, alchemy and even Government itself, the last of which I will not propose to discourse of, or meddle at all in, since it no ways belongs to my trade or vocation as the rest do, which, thanks to my God, I find much more safe, I think equally honest, and therefore more profitable.

But as to all the former, they have been so erroneously practised by many unlearned wretches, whom poverty and neediness for the most part (if not the restless itch of deceiving) has forced to straggle and wander in unknown paths, that even the professions themselves, though originally products of the most learned and wise men's laborious studies and experiences, and by them left a wealthy and glorious inheritance for ages to come, seem by this bastard race of quacks and cheats to have been run out of all wisdom, learning, perspicuousness & truth, with which they were so plentifully stocked, and now run into a repute of mere mists, imaginations, errors & deceits, such as in the management of these idle professors indeed they were.

You will therefore (I hope) Gentlemen, Ladies and others, deem it but just that I who for some years have, with all faithfulness and assiduity, courted these arts and received such signal favours from them that they have admitted me to the happy and full enjoyment of themselves & trusted me with their greatest secrets, should with an earnestness & concern more than ordinary take their parts against those impudent fops whose saucy, impertinent addresses and pretensions have brought such scandal upon their most immaculate honours and reputations.

Besides, I hope you will not think I could be so imprudent that if I had intended any such foul play myself, I should have given you so fair warning by my severe observations upon others. Qui alterum incusat probri, ipsum se intueri oportet. *Plaut.*

However, Gentlemen, in a world like this, where Virtue is so frequently exactly counterfeited and Hypocrisy so generally taken notice of that everyone armed with suspicion stands upon his guard against it, 'twill be very hard, for a stranger especially, to escape a censure: All I shall say for myself on this score is this, if I appear to anyone like a counterfeit, even for the sake of that chiefly ought I to be construed a true man, who is the counterfeit's example, his original, and that which he imploys his industry and pains to imitate

& copy. Is it, therefore, my fault if the cheat, by his wits and endeavours, makes himself so like me that consequently I cannot avoid resembling him? Consider, pray, the valiant and the coward, the wealthy merchant & the bankrupt, the politician and the fool; they are the same in many things & differ but in one alone: the valiant man holds up his head, looks confidently round about him, wears a sword, courts a lord's wife and owns it, so does the coward one only point of honour, and that's courage (which like a false metal one only trial can discover) makes the distinction.

The bankrupt walks the Exchange, buys bargains, draws bills & accepts them with the richest, whilst paper & credit are current coin; that which makes the difference is real cash, a great difference indeed, & yet but one, and that the last found out: and still till then the least perceived.

Now for the politician, he is a grave, deliberating, close, prying man; pray, are there not grave, deliberating, close, prying fools? If then the difference betwixt all these (though infinite in effect) be so nice in all appearance, will you expect it should be otherwise betwixt the false physician, astrologer &c. and the true? The first calls himself learned doctor, sends forth his bills, gives physic and counsel, tells and foretells; the other is bound to do just as much; 'tis only your experience must distinguish betwixt them, to which I willingly submit myself. I'll only say something to the honour of the mountebank, in case you discover me to be one.

Reflect a little what kind a creature 'tis: he is one, then, who is fain to supply some higher ability he pretends to with craft; he draws great companies to him, by undertaking strange things which can never be effected.

The politician (by his example no doubt) finding how the people are taken with specious miraculous impossibilities, plays the same game, protests, declares, promises I know not what things which he's sure can ne'er be brought about; the people believe, are deluded and pleased. The expectation of a future good, which shall never befall them, draws their eyes off a present evil; thus are they kept & established in subjection, peace & obedience, he in greatness, wealth and power; so you see the politician is, & must be, a mountebank in State affairs, and the mountebank no doubt (if he thrives) is an errant politician in physic.

But that I may not prove too tedious, I will proceed faithfully to inform you what are the things in which I pretend chiefly at this time to serve my country. . . .

Poems c. 1674–5

Timon

A. What, Timon! does old age begin t' approach,
That thus thou droop'st under a night's debauch?
Hast thou lost deep to needy rogues on tick,
Who ne'er could pay, and must be paid next week?
Timon. Neither, alas; but a dull dining sot
Seized me i' th' Mall, who just my name had got.
He runs upon me, cries, 'Dear rogue, I'm thine!
With me some wits of thy acquaintance dine.'
I tell him I'm engaged, but as a whore
With modesty enslaves her spark the more,
The longer I denied, the more he pressed.
At last I e'en consent to be his guest.

He takes me in his coach, and as we go,
Pulls out a libel of a sheet or two,
Insipid as the praise of pious queens
Or Shadwell's unassisted former scenes,
Which he admired, and praised at every line;
At last it was so sharp it must be mine.
I vowed I was no more a wit than he:
Unpractised and unblessed in poetry.
A song to Phyllis I perhaps might make,
But never rhymed but for my pintle's sake.
I envied no man's fortune nor his fame,
Nor ever thought of a revenge so tame.
He knew my style, he swore, and 'twas in vain
Thus to deny the issue of my brain.
Choked with his flattery, I no answer make,
But silent, leave him to his dear mistake,
Which he by this had spread o'er the whole town,

And me with an officious lie undone.
Of a well-meaning fool I'm most afraid,
Who sillily repeats what was well said.

But this was not the worst. When he came home,
He asked, 'Are Sedley, Buckhurst, Savile come?'
No, but there were above Halfwit and Huff,
Kickum and Dingboy. 'Oh, 'tis well enough!
They're all brave fellows,' cries mine host. 'Let's dine!
I long to have my belly full of wine.
They'll write and fight, I dare assure you:
They're men *tam Marte quam Mercurio.*'
I saw my error, but 'twas now too late:
No means nor hopes appear of a retreat.
Well, we salute, and each man takes his seat.
'Boy!' says my sot. 'Is my wife ready yet?'
A wife, good gods! a fop, and bullies too!
For one poor meal what must I undergo?

In comes my lady straight. She had been fair,
Fit to give love and to prevent despair,
But age, beauty's incurable disease,
Had left her more desire than power to please.
As cocks will strike although their spurs be gone,
She with her old blear eyes to smite begun.
Though nothing else, she in despite of time
Preserved the affectation of her prime:
However you begun, she brought in love,
And hardly from that subject would remove.
We chanced to speak of the French king's success;
My lady wondered much how heaven could bless
A man that loved two women at one time,
But more how he to them excused his crime.
She asked Huff if love's flame he never felt;
He answered bluntly, 'Do you think I'm gelt?'
She at his plainness smiled, then turned to me:
'Love in young minds precedes ev'n poetry:
You to that passion can no stranger be,
But wits are given to inconstancy.'

She had run on, I think, till now, but meat

Came up, and suddenly she took her seat.
I thought the dinner would make some amends,
When my good host cries out, 'Y' are all my friends!
Our own plain fare, and the best terse the Bull
Affords, I'll give you and your bellies full.
As for French kickshaws, sillery and champagne,
Ragouts and fricassees, in troth w' have none.'
Here's a good dinner towards, thought I, when straight
Up comes a piece of beef, full horseman's weight,
Hard as the arse of Mosely, under which
The coachman sweats as ridden by a witch;
A dish of carrots, each of them as long
As tool that to fair countess did belong,
Which her small pillow could not so well hide
But visitors his flaming head espied.
Pig, goose, and capon followed in the rear,
With all that country bumpkins call good cheer,
Served up with sauces, all of eighty-eight,
When our tough youth wrestled and threw the weight.
And now the bottle briskly flies about,
Instead of ice, wrapped up in a wet clout.
A brimmer follows the third bit we eat:
Small beer becomes our drink, and wine our meat.
The table was so large that in less space
A man might, safe, six old Italians place;
Each man had as much room as Porter, Blount,
Or Harris had in Cullen's bushel cunt.

And now the wine began to work, mine host
Had been a colonel; we must hear him boast,
Not of towns won, but an estate he lost
For the King's service, which indeed he spent
Whoring and drinking, but with good intent.
He talked much of a plot and money lent
In Cromwell's time. My lady, she
Complained our love was coarse, our poetry
Unfit for modest ears; small whores and players
Were of our harebrained youth the only cares,
Who were too wild for any virtuous league,

Too rotten to consummate the intrigue.
Falkland she praised, and Suckling's easy pen,
And seemed to taste their former parts again.
Mine host drinks to the best in Christendom,
And decently my lady quits the room.
    Left to ourselves, of several things we prate:
Some regulate the stage, and some the state.
Halfwit cries up my lord of Orrery:
Ah, how well Mustapha and Zanger die!
His sense so little forced that by one line
You may the other easily divine:
'And which is worse, if any worse can be,
He never said one word of it to me.'
There's fine poetry! You'd swear 'twere prose,
So little on the sense the rhymes impose.
'Damn me!' says Dingboy. 'In my mind, God's wounds,
Etherege writes airy songs and soft lampoons
The best of any man; as for your nouns,
Grammar, and rules of art, he knows 'em not,
Yet writ two talking plays without one plot.'
Huff was for Settle, and *Morocco* praised;
Said rumbling words, like drums, his courage raised:
'Whose broad-built bulks the boist'rous billows bear;
Safi and Salé, Mogador, Oran,
The famed Arzile, Alcazar, Tetuan.'
Was ever braver language writ by man?
Kickum for Crowne declared; said in romance
He had outdone the very wits of France:
Witness *Pandion* and his *Charles the Eighth*,
Where a young monarch, careless of his fate,
Though foreign troops and rebels shock his state,
Complains another sight afflicts him more,
Viz. 'the queen's galleys rowing from the shore,
Fitting their oars and tackling to be gone,
Whilst sporting waves smiled on the rising sun.'
Waves smiling on the sun? I'm sure *that's* new,
And 'twas well thought on, give the Devil his due.
Mine host, who had said nothing in an hour,

Rose up and praised the *Indian Emperor*:
'As if our old world modestly withdrew,
And here in private had brought forth a new.'
There are two lines! Who but *he* durst presume
To make th' old world a new withdrawing room,
Where of another world she's brought to bed?
What a brave midwife is a Laureate's head!

'But pox of all these scribblers! What d' ye think:
Will Souches this year any champagne drink?
Will Turenne fight him?' 'Without doubt,' says Huff,
'When they two meet, their meeting will be rough.'
'Damn me!' says Dingboy. 'The French cowards are.
They pay, but th' English, Scots, and Swiss make war.
In gaudy troops at a review they shine,
But dare not with the Germans battle join.
What now appears like courage is not so:
'Tis a short pride which from success does grow.
On their first blow they'll shrink into those fears
They showed at Cressy, Agincourt, Poitiers.
Their loss was infamous; honour so stained
Is by a nation not to be regained.'
'What they were then, I know not; now th' are brave.
He that denies it – lies and is a slave,'
Says Huff and frowned. Says Dingboy, 'That do I!'
And at that word at t' other's head let fly
A greasy plate, when suddenly they all
Together by the ears in parties fall:
Halfwit with Dingboy joins, Kickum with Huff.
Their swords were safe, and so we let them cuff
Till they, mine host, and I had all enough.
Their rage once over, they begin to treat,
And six fresh bottles must the peace complete.

I ran downstairs, with a vow nevermore
To drink beer-glass and hear the hectors roar.

Tunbridge Wells

At five this morn, when Phoebus raised his head

From Thetis' lap, I raised myself from bed,
And mounting steed, I trotted to the waters,
The rendezvous of fools, buffoons, and praters,
Cuckolds, whores, citizens, their wives and daughters.
  My squeamish stomach I with wine had bribed
To undertake the dose that was prescribed;
But turning head, a sudden cursèd view
That innocent provision overthrew,
And without drinking, made me purge and spew.
From coach and six a thing unwieldy rolled,
Whose lumber, cart more decently would hold.
As wise as calf it looked, as big as bully,
But handled, proves a mere Sir Nicholas Cully;
A bawling fop, a natural Nokes, and yet
He dares to censure as if he had wit.
To make him more ridiculous, in spite
Nature contrived the fool should be a knight.
Though he alone were dismal sight enough,
His train contributed to set him off,
All of his shape, all of the selfsame stuff.
No spleen or malice need on them be thrown:
Nature has done the business of lampoon,
And in their looks their characters has shown.
  Endeavouring this irksome sight to balk,
And a more irksome noise, their silly talk,
I silently slunk down t' th' Lower Walk.
But often when one would Charybdis shun,
Down upon Scylla 'tis one's fate to run,
For here it was my cursèd luck to find
As great a fop, though of another kind,
A tall stiff fool that walked in Spanish guise:
The buckram puppet never stirred its eyes,
But grave as owl it looked, as woodcock wise.
He scorns the empty talking of this mad age,
And speaks all proverbs, sentences, and adage;
Can with as much solemnity buy eggs
As a cabal can talk of their intrigues;
Master o' th' Ceremonies, yet can dispense

89

With the formality of talking sense.
From hence unto the upper end I ran,
Where a new scene of foppery began.
A tribe of curates, priests, canonical elves,
Fit company for none besides themselves,
Were got together. Each his distemper told,
Scurvy, stone, strangury; some were so bold
To charge the spleen to be their misery,
And on that wise disease brought infamy.
But none had modesty enough t' complain
Their want of learning, honesty, and brain,
The general diseases of that train.
These call themselves ambassadors of heaven,
And saucily pretend commissions given;
But should an Indian king, whose small command
Seldom extends beyond ten miles of land,
Send forth such wretched tools in an ambassage,
He'd find but small effects of such a message.
Listening, I found the cob of all this rabble
Pert Bays, with his importance comfortable.
He, being raised to an archdeaconry
By trampling on religion, liberty,
Was grown too great, and looked too fat and jolly,
To be disturbed with care and melancholy,
Though Marvell has enough exposed his folly.
He drank to carry off some old remains
His lazy dull distemper left in 's veins.
Let him drink on, but 'tis not a whole flood
Can give sufficient sweetness to his blood
To make his nature or his manners good.
Next after these, a fulsome Irish crew
Of silly Macs were offered to my view.
The things did talk, but th' hearing what they said
I did myself the kindness to evade.
Nature has placed these wretches beneath scorn:
They can't be called so vile as they are born.
Amidst the crowd next I myself conveyed,
For now were come, whitewash and paint being laid,

Mother and daughter, mistress and the maid,
And squire with wig and pantaloon displayed.
But ne'er could conventicle, play or fair
For a true medley, with this herd compare.
Here lords, knights, squires, ladies and countesses,
Chandlers, mum-bacon women, sempstresses
Were mixed together, nor did they agree
More in their humours than their quality.
  Here waiting for gallant, young damsel stood,
Leaning on cane, and muffled up in hood.
The would-be wit, whose business was to woo,
With hat removed and solemn scrape of shoe
Advanceth bowing, then genteelly shrugs,
And ruffled foretop into order tugs,
And thus accosts her: 'Madam, methinks the weather
Is grown much more serene since you came hither.
You influence the heavens; but should the sun
Withdraw himself to see his rays outdone
By your bright eyes, they would supply the morn,
And make a day before the day be born.'
With mouth screwed up, conceited winking eyes,
And breasts thrust forward, 'Lord, sir!' she replies.
'It is your goodness, and not my deserts,
Which makes you show this learning, wit, and parts.'
He, puzzled, bites his nail, both to display
The sparkling ring, and think what next to say,
And thus breaks forth afresh: 'Madam, egad!
Your luck at cards last night was very bad:
At cribbage fifty-nine, and the next show
To make the game, and yet to want those two.
God damn me, madam, I'm the son of a whore
If in my life I saw the like before!'
To peddler's stall he drags her, and her breast
With hearts and such-like foolish toys he dressed;
And then, more smartly to expound the riddle
Of all his prattle, gives her a Scotch fiddle.
  Tired with this dismal stuff, away I ran
Where were two wives, with girl just fit for man –

Short-breathed, with pallid lips and visage wan.
Some curtsies past, and the old compliment
Of being glad to see each other, spent,
With hand in hand they lovingly did walk,
And one began thus to renew the talk:
'I pray, good madam, if it may be thought
No rudeness, what cause was it hither brought
Your ladyship?' She, soon replying, smiled,
'We have a good estate, but have no child,
And I'm informed these wells will make a barren
Woman as fruitful as a cony warren.'
The first returned, 'For this cause I am come,
For I can have no quietness at home.
My husband grumbles though we have got one,
This poor young girl, and mutters for a son.
And this is grieved with headache, pangs, and throes;
Is full sixteen, and never yet had *those*.'
She soon replied, 'Get her a husband, madam:
I married at that age, and ne'er had had 'em;
Was just like her. Steel waters let alone:
A back of steel will bring 'em better down.'
And ten to one but they themselves will try
The same means to increase their family.
Poor foolish fribble, who by subtlety
Of midwife, truest friend to lechery,
Persuaded art to be at pains and charge
To give thy wife occasion to enlarge
Thy silly head! For here walk Cuff and Kick,
With brawny back and legs and potent prick,
Who more substantially will cure thy wife,
And on her half-dead womb bestow new life.
From these the waters got the reputation
Of good assistants unto generation.

Some warlike men were now got into th' throng,
With hair tied back, singing a bawdy song.
Not much afraid, I got a nearer view,
And 'twas my chance to know the dreadful crew.
They were cadets, that seldom can appear:

Damned to the stint of thirty pounds a year.
With hawk on fist, or greyhound led in hand,
The dogs and footboys sometimes they command.
But now, having trimmed a cast-off spavined horse,
With three hard-pinched-for guineas in their purse,
Two rusty pistols, scarf about the arse,
Coat lined with red, they here presume to swell:
This goes for captain, that for colonel.
So the Bear Garden ape, on his steed mounted,
No longer is a jackanapes accounted,
But is, by virtue of his trumpery, then
Called by the name of 'the young gentleman'.
   Bless me! thought I, what thing is man, that thus
In all his shapes, he is ridiculous?
Ourselves with noise of reason we do please
In vain: humanity's our worst disease.
Thrice happy beasts are, who, because they be
Of reason void, are so of foppery.
Faith, I was so ashamed that with remorse
I used the insolence to mount my horse;
For he, doing only things fit for his nature,
Did seem to me by much the wiser creature.

Upon His Leaving His Mistress

'Tis not that I am weary grown
Of being yours, and yours alone;
But with what face can I incline
To damn you to be only mine?
   You, whom some kinder power did fashion,
   By merit and by inclination,
   The joy at least of one whole nation.

Let meaner spirits of your sex
With humbler aims their thoughts perplex,
And boast if by their arts they can
Contrive to make *one* happy man;
   Whilst, moved by an impartial sense,

Favours like nature you dispense
With universal influence.

See, the kind seed-receiving earth
To every grain affords a birth.
On her no showers unwelcome fall;
Her willing womb retains 'em all.
    And shall my Celia be confined?
    No! Live up to thy mighty mind,
    And be the mistress of mankind.

The Fall

How blest was the created state
    Of man and woman, ere they fell,
Compared to our unhappy fate:
    We need not fear another hell.

Naked beneath cool shades they lay;
    Enjoyment waited on desire;
Each member did their wills obey,
    Nor could a wish set pleasure higher.

But we, poor slaves to hope and fear,
    Are never of our joys secure;
They lessen still as they draw near,
    And none but dull delights endure.

Then, Chloris, while I duly pay
    The nobler tribute of my heart,
Be not you so severe to say
    You love me for the frailer part.

The Mistress

An age in her embraces passed
    Would seem a winter's day,

Where life and light with envious haste
   Are torn and snatched away.

But oh, how slowly minutes roll
   When absent from her eyes,
That feed my love, which is my soul:
   It languishes and dies.

For then no more a soul, but shade,
   It mournfully does move
And haunts my breast, by absence made
   The living tomb of love.

You wiser men, despise me not
   Whose lovesick fancy raves
On shades of souls, and heaven knows what:
   Short ages live in graves.

Whene'er those wounding eyes, so full
   Of sweetness, you did see,
Had you not been profoundly dull,
   You had gone mad like me.

Nor censure us, you who perceive
   My best beloved and me
Sigh and lament, complain and grieve:
   You think we disagree.

Alas! 'tis sacred jealousy,
   Love raised to an extreme:
The only proof 'twixt her and me
   We love, and do not dream.

Fantastic fancies fondly move
   And in frail joys believe,
Taking false pleasure for true love;
   But pain can ne'er deceive.

Kind jealous doubts, tormenting fears,
    And anxious cares, when past,
Prove our hearts' treasure fixed and dear,
    And make us blest at last.

A Song

Absent from thee, I languish still;
    Then ask me not, when I return?
The straying fool 'twill plainly kill
    To wish all day, all night to mourn.

Dear! from thine arms then let me fly,
    That my fantastic mind may prove
The torments it deserves to try
    That tear my fixed heart from my love.

When, wearied with a world of woe,
    To thy safe bosom I retire
Where love and peace and truth does flow,
    May I contented there expire,

Lest, once more wandering from that heaven,
    I fall on some base heart unblest,
Faithless to thee, false, unforgiven,
    And lose my everlasting rest.

A Song of a Young Lady to Her Ancient Lover

Ancient person, for whom I
All the flattering youth defy,
Long be it ere thou grow old,
Aching, shaking, crazy, cold;
    But still continue as thou art,
    Ancient person of my heart.

On thy withered lips and dry,
Which like barren furrows lie,
Brooding kisses I will pour
Shall thy youthful heat restore
(Such kind showers in autumn fall,
And a second spring recall);
    Nor from thee will ever part,
    Ancient person of my heart.

Thy nobler part, which but to name
In our sex would be counted shame,
By age's frozen grasp possessed,
From [his] ice shall be released,
And soothed by my reviving hand,
In former warmth and vigour stand.
All a lover's wish can reach
For thy joy my love shall teach,
And for thy pleasure shall improve
All that art can add to love.
    Yet still I love thee without art,
    Ancient person of my heart.

Love and Life

All my past life is mine no more;
    The flying hours are gone,
Like transitory dreams given o'er
Whose images are kept in store
    By memory alone.

Whatever is to come is not:
    How can it then be mine?
The present moment's all my lot,
And that, as fast as it is got,
    Phyllis, is wholly thine.

Then talk not of inconstancy,
    False hearts, and broken vows;

If I, by miracle, can be
This livelong minute true to thee,
   'Tis all that heaven allows.

A Satire against Reason and Mankind

Were I (who to my cost already am
One of those strange, prodigious creatures, man)
A spirit free to choose, for my own share,
What case of flesh and blood I pleased to wear,
I'd be a dog, a monkey, or a bear,
Or anything but that vain animal
Who is so proud of being rational.
   The senses are too gross, and he'll contrive
A sixth, to contradict the other five,
And before certain instinct, will prefer
Reason, which fifty times for one does err:
Reason, an *ignis fatuus* in the mind,
Which, leaving light of nature, sense, behind,
Pathless and dangerous wandering ways it takes
Through error's fenny bogs and thorny brakes;
Whilst the misguided follower climbs with pain
Mountains of whimseys, heaped in his own brain;
Stumbling from thought to thought, falls headlong down
Into doubt's boundless sea, where, like to drown,
Books bear him up awhile, and make him try
To swim with bladders of philosophy;
In hopes still to o'ertake th' escaping light,
The vapour dances in his dazzling sight
Till, spent, it leaves him to eternal night.
Then old age and experience, hand in hand,
Lead him to death, and make him understand,
After a search so painful and so long,
That all his life he has been in the wrong.
Huddled in dirt the reasoning engine lies,
Who was so proud, so witty, and so wise.
   Pride drew him in, as cheats their bubbles catch,
And made him venture to be made a wretch.

His wisdom did his happiness destroy,
Aiming to know that world he should enjoy.
And wit was his vain, frivolous pretence
Of pleasing others at his own expense,
For wits are treated just like common whores:
First they're enjoyed, and then kicked out of doors.
The pleasure past, a threatening doubt remains
That frights th' enjoyer with succeeding pains.
Women and men of wit are dangerous tools,
And ever fatal to admiring fools:
Pleasure allures, and when the fops escape,
'Tis not that they're belov'd, but fortunate,
And therefore what they fear at heart, they hate.

    But now, methinks, some formal band and beard
Takes me to task. Come on, sir; I'm prepared.

    'Then, by your favour, anything that's writ
Against this gibing, jingling knack called wit
Likes me abundantly; but you take care
Upon this point, not to be too severe.
Perhaps my muse were fitter for this part,
For I profess I can be very smart
On wit, which I abhor with all my heart.
I long to lash it in some sharp essay,
But your grand indiscretion bids me stay
And turns my tide of ink another way.

    'What rage ferments in your degenerate mind
To make you rail at reason and mankind?
Blest, glorious man! to whom alone kind heaven
An everlasting soul has freely given,
Whom his great Maker took such care to make
That from himself he did the image take
And this fair frame in shining reason dressed
To dignify his nature above beast;
Reason, by whose aspiring influence
We take a flight beyond material sense,
Dive into mysteries, then soaring pierce
The flaming limits of the universe,
Search heaven and hell, find out what's acted there,

And give the world true grounds of hope and fear.'
   Hold, mighty man, I cry, all this we know
From the pathetic pen of Ingelo,
From Patrick's *Pilgrim*, Sibbes' soliloquies,
And 'tis this very reason I despise:
This supernatural gift, that makes a mite
Think he's the image of the infinite,
Comparing his short life, void of all rest,
To the eternal and the ever blest;
This busy, puzzling stirrer-up of doubt
That frames deep mysteries, then finds 'em out,
Filling with frantic crowds of thinking fools
Those reverend bedlams, colleges and schools;
Borne on whose wings, each heavy sot can pierce
The limits of the boundless universe;
So charming ointments make an old witch fly
And bear a crippled carcass through the sky.
'Tis this exalted power, whose business lies
In nonsense and impossibilities,
This made a whimsical philosopher
Before the spacious world, his tub prefer,
And we have modern cloistered coxcombs who
Retire to think, 'cause they have nought to do.
   But thoughts are given for action's government;
Where action ceases, thought's impertinent.
Our sphere of action is life's happiness,
And he who thinks beyond, thinks like an ass.
Thus, whilst against false reasoning I inveigh,
I own right reason, which I would obey:
That reason which distinguishes by sense
And gives us rules of good and ill from thence,
That bounds desires with a reforming will
To keep 'em more in vigour, not to kill.
Your reason hinders, mine helps to enjoy,
Renewing appetites yours would destroy.
My reason is my friend, yours is a cheat;
Hunger calls out, my reason bids me eat;
Perversely, yours your appetite does mock:

This asks for food, that answers, 'What's o'clock?'
This plain distinction, sir, your doubt secures:
'Tis not true reason I despise, but yours.

Thus I think reason righted, but for man,
I'll ne'er recant; defend him if you can.
For all his pride and his philosophy,
'Tis evident beasts are, in their degree,
As wise at least, and better far than he.
Those creatures are the wisest who attain,
By surest means, the ends at which they aim.
If therefore Jowler finds and kills his hares
Better than Meres supplies committee chairs,
Though one's a statesman, th' other but a hound,
Jowler, in justice, would be wiser found.

You see how far man's wisdom here extends;
Look next if human nature makes amends:
Whose principles most generous are, and just,
And to whose morals you would sooner trust.
Be judge yourself, I'll bring it to the test:
Which is the basest creature, man or beast?
Birds feed on birds, beasts on each other prey,
But savage man alone does man betray.
Pressed by necessity, they kill for food;
Man undoes man to do himself no good.
With teeth and claws by nature armed, they hunt
Nature's allowance, to supply their want.
But man, with smiles, embraces, friendship, praise,
Inhumanly his fellow's life betrays;
With voluntary pains works his distress,
Not through necessity, but wantonness.

For hunger or for love they fight and tear,
Whilst wretched man is still in arms for fear.
For fear he arms, and is of arms afraid,
By fear to fear successively betrayed;
Base fear, the source whence his best passions came:
His boasted honour, and his dear-bought fame;
That lust of power, to which he's such a slave,
And for the which alone he dares be brave;

To which his various projects are designed;
Which makes him generous, affable, and kind;
For which he takes such pains to be thought wise,
And screws his actions in a forced disguise,
Leading a tedious life in misery
Under laborious, mean hypocrisy.
Look to the bottom of his vast design,
Wherein man's wisdom, power, and glory join:
The good he acts, the ill he does endure,
'Tis all from fear, to make himself secure.
Merely for safety, after fame we thirst,
For all men would be cowards if they durst.
   And honesty's against all common sense:
Men must be knaves, 'tis in their own defence.
Mankind's dishonest; if you think it fair
Amongst known cheats to play upon the square,
You'll be undone.
Nor can weak truth your reputation save:
The knaves will all agree to call you knave.
Wronged shall he live, insulted o'er, oppressed,
Who dares be less a villain than the rest.
   Thus, sir, you see what human nature craves:
Most men are cowards, all men should be knaves.
The difference lies, as far as I can see,
Not in the thing itself, but the degree,
And all the subject matter of debate
Is only: Who's a knave of the first rate?

   All this with indignation have I hurled
At the pretending part of the proud world,
Who, swollen with selfish vanity, devise
False freedoms, holy cheats, and formal lies
Over their fellow slaves to tyrannize.
   But if in Court so just a man there be
(In Court a just man, yet unknown to me)
Who does his needful flattery direct,
Not to oppress and ruin, but protect
(Since flattery, which way soever laid,

Is still a tax on that unhappy trade);
If so upright a statesman you can find,
Whose passions bend to his unbiased mind,
Who does his arts and policies apply
To raise his country, not his family,
Nor, whilst his pride owned avarice withstands,
Receives close bribes through friends' corrupted hands –
  Is there a churchman who on God relies;
Whose life, his faith and doctrine justifies?
Not one blown up with vain prelatic pride,
Who, for reproof of sins, does man deride;
Whose envious heart makes preaching a pretence,
With his obstreperous, saucy eloquence,
To chide at kings, and rail at men of sense;
None of that sensual tribe whose talents lie
In avarice, pride, sloth, and gluttony;
Who hunt good livings, but abhor good lives;
Whose lust exalted to that height arrives
They act adultery with their own wives,
And ere a score of years completed be,
Can from the lofty pulpit proudly see
Half a large parish their own progeny;
Nor doting bishop who would be adored
For domineering at the council board,
A greater fop in business at fourscore,
Fonder of serious toys, affected more,
Than the gay, glittering fool at twenty proves
With all his noise, his tawdry clothes, and loves;
  But a meek, humble man of honest sense,
Who, preaching peace, does practise continence;
Whose pious life's a proof he does believe
Mysterious truths, which no man can conceive.
If upon earth there dwell such God-like men,
I'll here recant my paradox to them,
Adore those shrines of virtue, homage pay,
And, with the rabble world, their laws obey.
  If such there be, yet grant me this at least:
Man differs more from man, than man from beast.

A Letter from Artemisia in the Town to Chloe in the Country

Chloe,
        In verse by your command I write.
Shortly you'll bid me ride astride, and fight:
These talents better with our sex agree
Than lofty flights of dangerous poetry.
Amongst the men, I mean the men of wit
(At least they passed for such before they writ),
How many bold adventurers for the bays,
Proudly designing large returns of praise,
Who durst that stormy, pathless world explore,
Were soon dashed back and wrecked on the dull shore,
Broke of that little stock they had before!
How would a woman's tottering bark be tossed
Where stoutest ships, the men of wit, are lost?
When I reflect on this, I straight grow wise,
And my own self thus gravely I advise:

   Dear Artemisia, poetry's a snare;
Bedlam has many mansions; have a care.
Your muse diverts you, makes the reader sad:
You fancy you're inspired; he thinks you mad.
Consider, too, 'twill be discreetly done
To make yourself the fiddle of the town,
To find th'ill-humoured pleasure at their need,
Cursed if you fail, and scorned though you succeed!
Thus, like an arrant woman as I am,
No sooner well convinced writing's a shame,
That whore is scarce a more reproachful name
Than poetess –
Like men that marry, or like maids that woo,
'Cause 'tis the very worst thing they can do,
Pleased with the contradiction and the sin,
Methinks I stand on thorns till I begin.

   Y' expect at least to hear what loves have passed
In this lewd town, since you and I met last;
What change has happened of intrigues, and whether

The old ones last, and who and who's together.
But how, my dearest Chloe, shall I set
My pen to write what I would fain forget?
Or name that lost thing, love, without a tear,
Since so debauched by ill-bred customs here?
Love, the most generous passion of the mind,
The softest refuge innocence can find,
The safe director of unguided youth,
Fraught with kind wishes and secured by truth;
That cordial drop heaven in our cup has thrown
To make the nauseous draught of life go down;
On which one only blessing, God might raise
In lands of atheists, subsidies of praise,
For none did e'er so dull and stupid prove
But felt a god, and blessed his power in love –
This only joy for which poor we were made
Is grown, like play, to be an arrant trade.
The rooks creep in, and it has got of late
As many little cheats and tricks as that.

But what yet more a woman's heart would vex,
'Tis chiefly carried on by our own sex;
Our silly sex! who, born like monarchs free,
Turn gypsies for a meaner liberty,
And hate restraint, though but from infamy.
They call whatever is not common, nice,
And deaf to nature's rule or love's advice,
Forsake the pleasure to pursue the vice.
To an exact perfection they have wrought
The action, love; the passion is forgot.
'Tis below wit, they tell you, to admire,
And ev'n without approving, they desire.
Their private wish obeys the public voice;
'Twixt good and bad, whimsey decides, not choice.
Fashions grow up for taste; at forms they strike;
They know what they would have, not what they like.
Bovey's a beauty, if some few agree
To call him so; the rest to that degree
Affected are, that with their ears they see.

Where I was visiting the other night
Comes a fine lady, with her humble knight,
Who had prevailed on her, through her own skill,
At his request, though much against his will,
To come to London.
As the coach stopped, we heard her voice, more loud
Than a great-bellied woman's in a crowd,
Telling the knight that her affairs require
He, for some hours, obsequiously retire.
I think she was ashamed to have him seen:
Hard fate of husbands! The gallant had been,
Though a diseased, ill-favoured fool, brought in.
'Dispatch,' says she, 'that business you pretend,
Your beastly visit to your drunken friend!
A bottle ever makes you look so fine;
Methinks I long to smell you stink of wine!
Your country drinking breath's enough to kill:
Sour ale corrected with a lemon peel.
Prithee, farewell! We'll meet again anon.'
The necessary thing bows, and is gone.

She flies upstairs, and all the haste does show
That fifty antic postures will allow,
And then bursts out: 'Dear madam, am not I
The altered'st creature breathing? Let me die,
I find myself ridiculously grown,
Embarrassée with being out of town,
Rude and untaught like any Indian queen:
My country nakedness is strangely seen.

'How is love governed, love that rules the state,
And pray, who are the men most worn of late?
When I was married, fools were *à la mode*.
The men of wit were then held *incommode*,
Slow of belief, and fickle in desire,
Who, ere they'll be persuaded, must inquire
As if they came to spy, not to admire.
With searching wisdom, fatal to their ease,
They still find out why what may, should not please;
Nay, take themselves for injured when we dare

Make 'em think better of us than we are,
And if we hide our frailties from their sights,
Call us deceitful jilts and hypocrites.
They little guess, who at our arts are grieved,
The perfect joy of being well deceived:
Inquisitive as jealous cuckolds grow,
Rather than not be knowing, they will know
What, being known, creates their certain woe.
Women should these, of all mankind, avoid,
For wonder by clear knowledge is destroyed.
Woman, who is an arrant bird of night,
Bold in the dusk before a fool's dull sight,
Should fly when reason brings the glaring light.
　'But the kind, easy fool, apt to admire
Himself, trusts us; his follies all conspire
To flatter his, and favour our desire.
Vain of his proper merit, he with ease
Believes we love him best who best can please.
On him our gross, dull, common flatteries pass,
Ever most joyful when most made an ass.
Heavy to apprehend, though all mankind
Perceive us false, the fop concerned is blind,
Who, doting on himself,
Thinks everyone that sees him of his mind.
These are true women's men.'
　　　　　　　　　　　　Here forced to cease
Through want of breath, not will to hold her peace,
She to the window runs, where she had spied
Her much esteemed dear friend, the monkey, tied.
With forty smiles, as many antic bows,
As if 't had been the lady of the house,
The dirty, chattering monster she embraced,
And made it this fine, tender speech at last:
'Kiss me, thou curious miniature of man!
How odd thou art! how pretty! how japan!
Oh, I could live and die with thee!' Then on
For half an hour in compliment she run.
　I took this time to think what nature meant

When this mixed thing into the world she sent,
So very wise, yet so impertinent:
One who knew everything; who, God thought fit,
Should be an ass through choice, not want of wit;
Whose foppery, without the help of sense,
Could ne'er have rose to such an excellence.
Nature's as lame in making a true fop
As a philosopher; the very top
And dignity of folly we attain
By studious search and labour of the brain,
By observation, counsel and deep thought:
God never made a coxcomb worth a groat.
We owe that name to industry and arts:
An eminent fool must be a fool of parts.
And such a one was she, who had turned o'er
As many books as men; loved much, read more;
Had a discerning wit; to her was known
Everyone's fault and merit, but her own.
All the good qualities that ever blessed
A woman so distinguished from the rest,
Except discretion only, she possessed.

But now, '*Mon cher* dear Pug,' she cries, '*adieu!*'
And the discourse broke off does thus renew:
'You smile to see me, whom the world perchance
Mistakes to have some wit, so far advance
The interest of fools, that I approve
Their merit, more than men's of wit, in love.
But, in our sex, too many proofs there are
Of such whom wits undo, and fools repair.
This, in my time, was so observed a rule
Hardly a wench in town but had her fool.
The meanest common slut, who long was grown
The jest and scorn of every pit buffoon,
Had yet left charms enough to have subdued
Some fop or other, fond to be thought lewd.
Foster could make an Irish lord a Nokes,
And Betty Morris had her City cokes.
A woman's ne'er so ruined but she can

Be still revenged on her undoer, man;
How lost soe'er, she'll find some lover, more
A lewd, abandoned fool than she a whore.

'That wretched thing Corinna, who had run
Through all the several ways of being undone,
Cozened at first by love, and living then
By turning the too dear-bought trick on men –
Gay were the hours, and winged with joys they flew,
When first the town her early beauties knew;
Courted, admired, and loved, with presents fed;
Youth in her looks, and pleasure in her bed;
Till fate, or her ill angel, thought it fit
To make her dote upon a man of wit,
Who found 'twas dull to love above a day;
Made his ill-natured jest, and went away.
Now scorned by all, forsaken and oppressed,
She's a *memento mori* to the rest;
Diseased, decayed, to take up half a crown
Must mortgage her long scarf and manteau gown.
Poor creature! who, unheard of as a fly,
In some dark hole must all the winter lie,
And want and dirt endure a whole half year
That for one month she tawdry may appear.

'In Easter Term she gets her a new gown,
When my young master's worship comes to town,
From pedagogue and mother just set free,
The heir and hopes of a great family;
Which, with strong ale and beef, the country rules,
And ever since the Conquest have been fools.
And now, with careful prospect to maintain
This character, lest crossing of the strain
Should mend the booby breed, his friends provide
A cousin of his own to be his bride.
And thus set out
With an estate, no wit, and a young wife
(The solid comforts of a coxcomb's life),
Dunghill and pease forsook, he comes to town,
Turns spark, learns to be lewd, and is undone.

Nothing suits worse with vice than want of sense:
Fools are still wicked at their own expense.
   'This o'ergrown schoolboy lost Corinna wins,
And at first dash to make an ass begins:
Pretends to like a man who has not known
The vanities nor vices of the town;
Fresh in his youth, and faithful in his love;
Eager of joys which he does seldom prove;
Healthful and strong, he does no pains endure
But what the fair one he adores can cure;
Grateful for favours, does the sex esteem,
And libels none for being kind to him;
Then of the lewdness of the times complains:
Rails at the wits and atheists, and maintains
'Tis better than good sense, than power or wealth,
To have a love untainted, youth, and health.
   'The unbred puppy, who had never seen
A creature look so gay or talk so fine,
Believes, then falls in love, and then in debt;
Mortgages all, ev'n to the ancient seat,
To buy this mistress a new house for life;
To give her plate and jewels, robs his wife.
And when t' th' height of fondness he is grown,
'Tis time to poison him, and all's her own.
Thus meeting in her common arms his fate,
He leaves her bastard heir to his estate,
And, as the race of such an owl deserves,
His own dull lawful progeny he starves.
   'Nature, who never made a thing in vain,
But does each insect to some end ordain,
Wisely contrived kind keeping fools, no doubt,
To patch up vices men of wit wear out.'
Thus she ran on two hours, some grains of sense
Still mixed with volleys of impertinence.
   But now 'tis time I should some pity show
To Chloe, since I cannot choose but know
Readers must reap the dullness writers sow.
By the next post such stories I will tell

As, joined with these, shall to a volume swell,
As true as heaven, more infamous than hell.
But you are tired, and so am I.

                                    Farewell.

The Disabled Debauchee

As some brave admiral, in former war
    Deprived of force, but pressed with courage still,
Two rival fleets appearing from afar,
    Crawls to the top of an adjacent hill;

From whence, with thoughts full of concern, he views
    The wise and daring conduct of the fight,
Whilst each bold action to his mind renews
    His present glory and his past delight;

From his fierce eyes flashes of fire he throws,
    As from black clouds when lightning breaks away;
Transported, thinks himself amidst the foes,
    And absent, yet enjoys the bloody day;

So, when my days of impotence approach,
    And I'm by pox and wine's unlucky chance
Forced from the pleasing billows of debauch
    On the dull shore of lazy temperance,

My pains at least some respite shall afford
    While I behold the battles you maintain
When fleets of glasses sail about the board,
    From whose broadsides volleys of wit shall rain.

Nor let the sight of honourable scars,
    Which my too forward valour did procure,
Frighten new-listed soldiers from the wars:
    Past joys have more than paid what I endure.

111

Should any youth (worth being drunk) prove nice,
  And from his fair inviter meanly shrink,
'Twill please the ghost of my departed vice
  If, at my counsel, he repent and drink.

Or should some cold-complexioned sot forbid,
  With his dull morals, our bold night-alarms,
I'll fire his blood by telling what I did
  When I was strong and able to bear arms.

I'll tell of whores attacked, their lords at home;
  Bawds' quarters beaten up, and fortress won;
Windows demolished, watches overcome;
  And handsome ills by my contrivance done.

Nor shall our love-fits, Chloris, be forgot,
  When each the well-looked linkboy strove t' enjoy,
And the best kiss was the deciding lot
  Whether the boy fucked you, or I the boy.

With tales like these I will such thoughts inspire
  As to important mischief shall incline:
I'll make him long some ancient church to fire,
  And fear no lewdness he's called to by wine.

Thus, statesmanlike, I'll saucily impose,
  And safe from action, valiantly advise;
Sheltered in impotence, urge you to blows,
  And being good for nothing else, be wise.

Upon Nothing

Nothing! thou elder brother even to Shade:
Thou hadst a being ere the world was made,
And well fixed, art alone of ending not afraid.

Ere Time and Place were, Time and Place were not,

When primitive Nothing Something straight begot;
Then all proceeded from the great united What.

Something, the general attribute of all,
Severed from thee, its sole original,
Into thy boundless self must undistinguished fall;

Yet Something did thy mighty power command,
And from thy fruitful Emptiness's hand
Snatched men, beasts, birds, fire, water, air, and land.

Matter, the wicked'st offspring of thy race,
By Form assisted, flew from thy embrace,
And rebel Light obscured thy reverend dusky face.

With Form and Matter, Time and Place did join;
Body, thy foe, with these did leagues combine
To spoil thy peaceful realm, and ruin all thy line;

But turncoat Time assists the foe in vain,
And bribed by thee, destroys their short-lived reign,
And to thy hungry womb drives back thy slaves again.

Though mysteries are barred from laic eyes,
And the divine alone with warrant pries
Into thy bosom, where the truth in private lies,

Yet this of thee the wise may truly say:
Thou from the virtuous nothing dost delay,
And to be part of thee the wicked wisely pray.

Great Negative, how vainly would the wise
Inquire, define, distinguish, teach, devise,
Didst thou not stand to point their blind philosophies!

Is or Is Not, the two great ends of Fate,
And True or False, the subject of debate,
That perfect or destroy the vast designs of state –

When they have racked the politician's breast,
Within thy bosom most securely rest,
And when reduced to thee, are least unsafe and best.

But Nothing, why does Something still permit
That sacred monarchs should in council sit
With persons highly thought at best for nothing fit,

While weighty Something modestly abstains
From princes' coffers, and from statesmen's brains,
And Nothing there like stately Nothing reigns?

Nothing! who dwellst with fools in grave disguise,
For whom they reverend shapes and forms devise,
Lawn sleeves and furs and gowns, when they like thee look wise,

French truth, Dutch prowess, British policy,
Hibernian learning, Scotch civility,
Spaniards' dispatch, Danes' wit are mainly seen in thee;

The great man's gratitude to his best friend,
Kings' promises, whores' vows – towards thee they bend,
Flow swiftly into thee, and in thee ever end.

5

'A Man Half in the Grave'

1675/6   *6 January*. Baptism of Malet, his fourth child.
      March. First performances of Etherege's *The Man of Mode*.
      17 June. Rochester, Etherege and others involved in a murderous affray at Epsom.

1678   *6 September*. Titus Oates laid the 'Popish Plot' before Sir Edmund Berry Godfrey.

1678/9   *Winter*. Rochester engaged in philosophical discussions with the deist Charles Blount, which were resumed in February 1679/80.

1679   *October*. Rochester began his conversations with Gilbert Burnet, later Bishop of Salisbury.

1680   *March*. At Newmarket Races with the king.
      April. Rode to Somerset. Brought by coach to Woodstock in a state of collapse.
      26 July. Died at the High Lodge, Woodstock Park.

Rochester as Dorimant

[Of Etherege's *The Man of Mode, or Sir Fopling Flutter* (1676) John Dennis wrote: 'Now I remember very well that upon the first acting this comedy it was generally believed to be an agreeable representation of the persons of condition of both sexes, both in Court and Town; and that all the world was charmed with Dorimont [*sic*]; and that it was unanimously agreed that he had in him several of the qualities of Wilmot, Earl of Rochester, as, his wit, his spirit, his amorous temper, the charms that he had for the fair sex, his falsehood and his inconstancy; the agreeable manner of his chiding his servants, which the late Bishop of Salisbury takes notice of in his Life; and lastly, his repeating, on every occasion, the verses of

Waller, for whom that noble lord had a very particular esteem; witness his Imitation of the Tenth Satire of the First book of Horace:

> Waller, by Nature for the Bays designed,
> With spirit, force, and fancy unconfined,
> In panegyric is above mankind.'

Defence of Sir Fopling Flutter, 1722]

The Man of Mode, or Sir Fopling Flutter

Act One, Scene One

A dressing room. A table covered with a toilet, clothes laid ready.
Enter DORIMANT, *in his gown and slippers, with a note in his hand made up, repeating verses.*

DORIMANT: *Now for some ages had the pride of Spain*
Made the sun shine on half the world in vain.

[*Then looking on the note*] 'For Mrs Loveit.' What a dull, insipid thing is a billet doux written in cold blood, after the heat of the business is over! It is a tax upon good nature which I have here been labouring to pay, and have done it, but with as much regret as ever fanatic paid the Royal Aid or church duties. 'Twill have the same fate, I know, that all my notes to her have had of late, 'twill not be thought kind enough. Faith, women are i' the right when they jealously examine our letters, for in them we always first discover our decay of passion. – Hey !– Who waits ? –

[*Enter* HANDY.]

HANDY: Sir –

DORIMANT: Call a footman.

HANDY: None of 'em are come yet.

DORIMANT: Dogs! Will they ever lie snoring abed till noon?

HANDY: 'Tis all one, sir: if they're up, you indulge 'em so, they're ever poaching after whores all the morning.

DORIMANT: Take notice henceforward, who's wanting in his duty, the next clap he gets, he shall rot for an example. What vermin are those chattering without?

HANDY: Foggy Nan, the orange-woman, and swearing Tom, the shoemaker.

DORIMANT: Go, call in that overgrown jade with the flasket of guts before her. Fruit is refreshing in a morning.

[*Exit* HANDY.]

> *It is not that I love you less*
> *Than when before your feet I lay.*

[*Enter* ORANGE-WOMAN.]

How now, double-tripe, what news do you bring?

ORANGE-WOMAN: News! Here's the best fruit has come to town t'year. Gad, I was up before four a clock this morning and bought all the choice i' the market.

DORIMANT: The nasty refuse of your shop.

ORANGE-WOMAN: You need not make mouths at it, I assure you, 'tis all culled ware.

DORIMANT: The citizens buy better on a holiday in their walk to Tottenham.

ORANGE-WOMAN: Good or bad, 'tis all one; I never knew you commend anything. Lord, would the ladies had heard you talk of 'em as I have done: here, bid your man give me an angel. [*Sets down the fruit.*]

DORIMANT: Give the bawd her fruit again.

ORANGE-WOMAN: Well, on my conscience, there never was the likes of you. God's my life, I had almost forgot to tell you, there is a young gentlewoman, lately come to town with her mother, that is so taken with you.

DORIMANT: Is she handsome?

ORANGE-WOMAN: Nay, Gad, there are few finer women, I tell you but so, and a hugeous fortune they say. Here, eat this peach, it comes from the stone, 'tis better than any Newington y'have tasted.

DORIMANT: This fine woman, I'll lay my life, is some awkward, [*taking the peach*] ill-fashioned country toad, who, not having above four dozen of black hairs on her head, has adorned her baldness with a large white fruz, that she may look sparkishly in the forefront of the King's Box at an old play.

ORANGE-WOMAN: Gad, you'd change your note quickly if you did but see her.

DORIMANT: How came she to know me?

ORANGE-WOMAN: She saw you yesterday at the Change. She told me you came and fooled with the woman at the next shop.

DORIMANT: I remember there was a mask observed me indeed. Fooled, did she say?

ORANGE-WOMAN: Ay, I vow she told me twenty things you said, too, and acted with her head and with her body so like you –

Rochester Begins to Write a Comedy

Scene One

Mr DAINTY's *chamber. Enter* DAINTY *in his nightgown singing –*

DAINTY: *J'ai l'amour dans le coeur et la rage dans les os* – I am confident I shall never sleep again & 't were no great matter if it did not make me look thin, for naturally I hate to be so long absent from myself, as one is in a manner those seven dull hours he snores away, & yet methinks not to sleep till the sun rise is an odd effect of my disease & makes the night tedious without a woman. Reading would relieve me, but books treat of other men's affairs, & to me that's ever tiresome. Beside, I seldom have candle, but I am resolved to write some love-passages of my life. They will make a pretty novel, & when my boy buys a link, it shall burn by me when I go to bed, while I divert myself with reading my own story, which will be pleasant enough. – Boy!

BOY [*enters*]: Sir!

DAINTY: Who knocked at door just now? Was it some woman?

BOY: Mrs Mannours' maid, sir, with a posset for you.

DAINTY: And you never brought her up, you rascal? How can you be so ill bred & belong to me? See who knocks there. Some other woman.

  [*Exit* BOY.]

This Mrs Mannours' fondness of me is very useful, for besides the good things she always sends me & money I borrow of her sometimes, I have a further prospect, Sir Lionel's daughters, which are in her charge. Both like me, but the youngest I pitch upon, & because I can't marry 'em both, my young nobility Mr

Squabb shall have the other sister, but I'll trouble him afterwards. Thus I'll raise my fortune, which is all I want, for I am an agreeable man and everybody likes me.

[*Enter* BOY.]

BOY: 'Tis Mr Squabb, sir.

DAINTY: Call him up, but comb your periwig first. Let me comb it – you are the laziest sloven.

[The fragment ends here. It is to be found, in Rochester's hand, among the Portland MSS. in Nottingham University Library (MS. PwV 31).]

Affray at Epsom

Mr Downs is dead. The Lord Rochester doth abscond, and so doth Etheridge and Capt. Bridges who occasioned the riot Sunday sennight. They were tossing some fiddlers in a blanket for refusing to play, and a barber, upon the noise, going to see what the matter, they seized upon him, and, to free himself from them, he offered to carry them to the handsomest woman in Epsom and directed them to the constable's house, who demanding what they came for, [they] told him a whore and, he refusing to let them in, they broke open his doors and broke his head and beat him very severely. At last he made his escape, called his watch, and Etheridge made a submissive oration to them and so far appeased them that the constable dismissed his watch. But presently after the Lord Rochester drew upon the constable. Mr Downs, to prevent his pass, seized on him, the constable cried out murther and, the watch returning, one came behind Mr Downs and with a sprittle staff cleft his skull. The Lord Rochester and the rest run away and Downs, having no sword, snatched up a stick and striking at them, they run him into the side with a half pike and so bruised his arm that he was never able to stir it after. . . .

Charles Hatton to his brother, 29 June 1676; E. M. Thompson, *Correspondence of the Family of Hatton*, I, London, 1878, p. 133

A Stabbing

Whitehall, May 24, 1677.

Last night also, Du Puis, a French cook in the Mall, was stabbed for some pert answer by one Mr Floyd, and because my Lord Rochester and my Lord Lumley were supping in the same house, though in both different rooms and companies, the good nature of the town has reported it all this day that his Lordship was the stabber. He desired me therefore to write to you to stop that report from going northward, for he says if it once get as far as York the truth will not be believed under two or three years.

Henry Savile to Viscount Halifax; *Savile Correspondence*, ed. W. D. Cooper, London, 1858, p. 58

'A Man Half in the Grave'

To the Honourable
Mr Henry Savile

[July, 1678]

Were I as idle as ever, which I should not fail of being, if health permitted, I would write a small romance and make the Sun with his dishevelled rays gild the tops of the palaces in Leather Lane: Then should those vile enchanters Barten and Ginman lead forth their illustrious captives in chains of quicksilver, and confining 'em by charms to the loathsome banks of a dead lake of diet-drink, you, as my friend, should break the horrid silence and speak the most passionate fine things that ever heroic lover uttered; which being softly and sweetly replied to by Mrs Roberts, should rudely be interrupted by the envious F — . Thus would I lead the mournful tale along, till the gentle reader bathed with the tribute of his eyes the names of such unfortunate lovers – and this, I take it, would be a most excellent way of celebrating the memories of my most pocky friends, companions and mistresses. But it is a miraculous thing (as the wise have it) when a man half in the grave cannot leave off playing the fool and the buffoon; but so it falls out to my comfort:

For at this moment I am in a damned relapse, brought by a fever, the stone, and some ten diseases more, which have deprived me of the power of crawling, which I happily enjoyed some days ago; and now, I fear, I must fall, that it may be fulfilled which was long since written for instruction in a good old ballad,

> But he who lives not wise and sober
> Falls with the leaf still in October.

About which time, in all probability, there may be a period added to the ridiculous being of

Your humble servant,

ROCHESTER.

> *Familiar Letters: Written by the Right Honourable, John, late Earl of Rochester, to the Honourable Henry Savile, Esq.*, London, 1697, pp. 12, 13

To His Son

Charles, I take it very kindly that you write to me (though seldom) & wish heartily you would behave yourself so as that I might show how much I love you without being ashamed; Obedience to your grandmother & those who instruct you in good things, is the way to make you happy here and for ever; avoid idleness, scorn lying, and God will bless you, for which I pray.

British Museum, Harleian MS. 7003

'In His Later Years'

(i)

In his later years he read books of history more.

> Gilbert Burnet, *Some Passages of the Life and Death of the Right Honourable John Earl of Rochester*, London, 1680, p. 27

I must not here forget that a considerable time before his last sickness his wit began to take a more serious bent and to frame and fashion itself to public business; he began to inform himself of the wisdom of our laws and the excellent constitution of the English Government, and to speak in the House of Peers with general approbation; he was inquisitive of all kinds of histories that concerned England, both ancient and modern, and set himself to read the Journals of Parliament Proceedings. In effect, he seemed to study nothing more than which way to make that great understanding God had given him most useful to his country, and I am confident, had he lived, his riper age would have served it as much as his youth had diverted it.

> Preface by 'one of his friends' (i.e. Robert Wolseley) to *Valentinian: a Tragedy. As 'tis Altered by the late Earl of Rochester and Acted at the Theatre Royal*, London, 1685

Rochester Speaks in the House of Lords, 1678

Mr Speaker,

Sir, although it hath been said that no good Protestant can speak against this Bill, yet, sir, I cannot forbear to offer some objections against it. I do not know that any of the King's murderers were condemned without being heard; and must we deal thus with the brother of our King? It is such a severe way of proceeding that I think we cannot answer it to the world; and therefore it would consist much better with the justice of the House to impeach him and try him in a formal way, and then cut off his head if he deserve it. I will not offer dispute the power of Parliaments; but I question whether this law, if made, would be good in itself. Some laws have a natural weakness with them; I think that by which the old Long Parliament carried on their rebellion was judged afterward void in law, because there was a power given which could not be taken from the Crown. For aught I know, when you have made this law it may have the same flaw in it: If not, I am confident there are a loyal

party which will never obey but will think themselves bound by
their oath of allegiance and duty to pay obedience to the Duke, if
ever he should come to be King, which must occasion a civil war.
And, sir, I do not find that the proviso that was ordered to be added
for the security of the Duke's children is made strong enough to
secure them, according to the debate of the House, it being liable
to many objections, and the more because the words *Presumptive
Heir of the Crown* are industriously left out, though much insisted
upon when debated here in the House. Upon the whole matter my
humble motion is, that the Bill may be thrown out.

*A Further Collection of the most Remarkable Speeches in
Both Houses of Parliament* (*The Works of George
Villiers, late Duke of Buckingham*, II, London, 1715,
pp. 271–3)

From the Diary of the Earl of Anglesey

Sept. 1, 1679. The King having slept well I came with my son
by Nickham home to Blechington, 33 m., and found all well and the
2 Lady Rochesters and much other company here, and others came
after.

Sept. 16, 1679. Spent the morning at home in business and con-
verse, the afternoon at the race for Woodstock Plate, which the
Earl of Rochester's gray won.

British Museum, Add. MS. 18730

Poems *c.* 1676–80

Dialogue

Nell Gwyn When to the King I bid good morrow
           With tongue in mouth and hand on tarse,
       Portsmouth may rend her cunt for sorrow,
        And Mazarin may kiss mine arse.

The Duchess of Portsmouth
>   When England's monarch's on my belly,
>   With prick in cunt, though double crammed,
>   Fart of mine arse for small whore Nelly,
>   And great whore Mazarin be damned.

The King   When on Portsmouth's lap I lay my head,
>   And Knight does sing her bawdy song,
>   I envy not George Porter's bed,
>   Nor the delights of Madam Long.

The People   Now heavens preserve our faith's defender
>   From Paris plots and Roman cunt;
>   From Mazarin, that new pretender,
>   And from that *politique*, Grammont.

To the Postboy

Rochester   Son of a whore, God damn you! can you tell
>   A peerless peer the readiest way to Hell?
>   I've outswilled Bacchus, sworn of my own make
>   Oaths would fright Furies and make Pluto quake;
>   I've swived more whores more ways than Sodom's walls
>   E'er knew, or the College of Rome's Cardinals.
>   Witness heroic scars – Look here, ne'er go! –
>   Cerecloths and ulcers from the top to toe!
>   Frighted at my own mischiefs, I have fled
>   And bravely left my life's defender dead;
>   Broke houses to break chastity, and dyed
>   That floor with murder which my lust denied.
>   Pox on 't, why do I speak of these poor things?
>   I have blasphemed my God, and libelled Kings!
>   The readiest way to Hell – Come, quick!

Boy   Ne'er stir:
>   The readiest way, my Lord, 's by Rochester.

Impromptu on Charles II

God bless our good and gracious King,

124

Whose promise none relies on;
Who never said a foolish thing,
Nor ever did a wise one.

Epilogue to *Circe*

Some few, from wit, have this true maxim got,
That *'tis still better to be pleased than not*,
And therefore never their own torment plot;
While the malicious critics still agree
To loathe each play they come, and pay, to see.
The first know 'tis a meaner part of sense
To find a fault than taste an excellence;
Therefore they praise and strive to like, while these
Are dully vain of being hard to please.
Poets and women have an equal right
To hate the dull, who, dead to all delight,
Feel pain alone, and have no joy but spite.
'Twas impotence did first this vice begin:
Fools censure wit as old men rail of sin,
Who envy pleasure which they cannot taste
And, good for nothing, would be wise at last.
Since therefore to the women it appears
That all these enemies of wit are theirs,
Our poet the dull herd no longer fears.
Whate'er his fate may prove, 'twill be his pride
To stand or fall with beauty on his side.

Seneca's *Troades*, Act II, Chorus

After death nothing is, and nothing, death:
The utmost limit of a gasp of breath.
Let the ambitious zealot lay aside
His hopes of heaven, whose faith is but his pride;
    Let slavish souls lay by their fear,

Nor be concerned which way nor where
After this life they shall be hurled.
Dead, we become the lumber of the world,
And to that mass of matter shall be swept
Where things destroyed with things unborn are kept.
Devouring time swallows us whole;
Impartial death confounds body and soul.
For Hell and the foul fiend that rules
God's everlasting fiery jails
(Devised by rogues, dreaded by fools),
With his grim, grisly dog that keeps the door,
Are senseless stories, idle tales,
Dreams, whimseys, and no more.

This last poem Rochester sent to Charles Blount and received the following reply:

Ludgate Hill, Feb. 7th [1679/80]

My Lord,
I had the honour yesterday to receive from the hands of an humble servant of your Lordship's your most incomparable version of that passage of Seneca's, where he begins with, — *Post mortem nihil est, ipsaque mors nihil,* &c. — and must confess, with your Lordship's pardon, that I cannot but esteem the translation to be, in some measure, a confutation of the original; since what less than a divine and immortal mind could have produced what you have there written? Indeed, the hand that wrote it may become *lumber,* but sure, the spirit that dictated it can never be so: No, my Lord, your mighty genius is a most sufficient argument of its own immortality; and more prevalent with me than all the harangues of the parsons or sophistry of the schoolmen. No subject whatever has more entangled and ruffled the thoughts of the wisest men than this concerning our future state. . . .

Charles Blount, *The Oracles of Reason (Miscellaneous Works,* London, 1695, pp. 117, 118)

John Cary to Sir Ralph Verney

And I grow old & infirm, and others' business is so much upon me. Especially my Lord Rochester's hath been & is like to be very troublesome, so as I cannot look to anything for myself. . . .

[4 January 1680]

The Verney Papers, Claydon, Bucks.

'I am No Atheist'

When my Lord came to Oxford he soon grew debauched; yet some time before his death he plainly told Mr Giffard, who went to see him, that he was no atheist. The occasion was this. Says his Lordship, *Mr Giffard, I wonder you will not come and visit me oftener. I have a great respect for you and I should be extremely glad of your frequent conversation.* Says Mr Giffard (who could say anything to him), *My Lord, I am a clergyman. Your Lordship has a very ill character of being a debauched man and an atheist, & 'twill not look well in me to keep company with your Lordship as long as this character lasts, and as long as you continue this course of life. Mr Giffard,* says my Lord, *I have been guilty of extravagances, but I will assure you I am no atheist,* with other words to the same purpose.

16 November 1711; Thomas Hearne, *Remarks and Collections*, III, Oxford, 1889, p. 263

A Winter's Conversation

(i)

I was called on to assist many who lay a dying, particularly one with whom Wilmot, E[arl] of Rochester, had an ill concern. He heard that in a long attendance on her I treated her neither with a slack indulgence nor an affrighting severity, upon that he sent for me and in many discourses with him I saw into the depths of Satan, and by a winter's conversation, generally once a week, I went through much ground with him, and as he owned to me I subdued his understanding, but the touching his heart was that which God reserved to himself and which followed some time after that. He had been a malicious observer of the applications the Clergy made at Court for preferment, and fortified himself and others with prejudices against religion, by the observations he made on their behaviour, and this made him so partial to me because he observed nothing of aspiring to preferment in me. He told me he said to King Charles, after the 1st. Volume of my History of the Reformation came out, he wondered why he would use a writer of history ill, for such people can revenge themselves. The King answered I durst say nothing while he was alive, when he was dead he should not be the worse for what I said. He gave me very strange impressions of that King and indeed the whole Court.

> Gilbert Burnet, *History of my own Time*, Supplement (Bodleian Add. MSS. D24), ed. H. C. Foxcroft, Oxford, 1902, pp. 486, 487

(ii)

The occasion that led me into so particular a knowledge of him was an intimation given me by a gentleman of his acquaintance of his desire to see me. This was some time in October, 1679, when he was slowly recovering out of a great disease. He had understood that I often attended on one well known to him that died the summer before; he was also then entertaining himself in that low state of his health, with the first part of the *History of the Reformation*, then newly come out, with which he seemed not ill pleased: and we had accidentally met in two or three places some time before. These were the motives that led him to call for my company. After I had waited on him once or twice, he grew into that freedom with me as to open to me all his thoughts, both of religion and morality: and to give me a full view of his past life: and seemed not uneasy at my frequent visits. So till he went from London, which was in the beginning of April, I waited on him often.

> Gilbert Burnet, *Some Passages of the Life and Death of*

the Right Honourable John Earl of Rochester, London, 1680, Preface (unnumbered pages)

(iii)

I followed him with such arguments as I saw were most likely to prevail with him: and my not urging other reasons proceeded not from any distrust I had of their force but from the necessity of using those that were most proper for him. He was then in a low state of health and seemed to be slowly recovering of a great disease: He was in the milk-diet and apt to fall into hectical fits; any accident weakened him, so that he thought he could not live long; and when he went from London he said he believed he should never come to town more. Yet during his being in town he was so well that he went often abroad and had great vivacity of spirit. So that he was under no decay as either darkened or weakened his understanding, nor was he any way troubled with the spleen or vapours, or under the power of melancholy. What he was then compared to what he had been formerly, I could not so well judge, who had seen him but twice before. Others have told me they perceived no difference in his parts. This I mention more particularly, that it may not be thought that melancholy or the want of spirits made him more inclined to receive any impressions; for indeed I never discovered any such thing in him.

Gilbert Burnet, *Some Passages of the Life and Death of the Right Honourable John Earl of Rochester*, London, 1680, pp. 33, 34

At Woodstock in May

Upon my first visit to him, (*May 26.*) just at his return from his journey out of the West, he most gladly received me, shewed me extraordinary respects upon the score of mine office, *thanked God, who had in mercy and good providence sent me to him, who so much needed my prayers and counsels; acknowledging how unworthily heretofore he had treated that order of men, reproaching them that they were proud, and prophesied only for rewards; but now he had learnt how to value them; that he esteemed them the servants of the most High God, who were to shew him the way to everlasting life.*

At the same time I found him labouring under strange trouble and conflicts of mind, his spirit wounded, and his conscience full of terrors. Upon his journey, he told me, *he had been arguing with greater vigour against God and Religion than ever he had done in his life time before, and that he was resolved to run 'em down with all the arguments and spite in the world, but,* like the great Convert St Paul, *he found it hard to kick against the pricks.* For God at that time had so struck his heart by his immediate hand, that presently he argued as strongly for God and Virtue as before he had done against it. That God strangely opened his heart, creating in his mind most awful and tremendous thoughts and ideas of the Divine Majesty, with a delightful contemplation of the Divine Nature and Attributes, and of the loveliness of Religion and Virtue. *I never* (said he) *was advanced thus far towards happiness in my life before, though upon the commissions of some sins extraordinary I have had some checks and warnings considerable from within, but still struggled with 'em, and so wore them off again.* The most observable that I remember was this: *One day at an atheistical meeting, at a person of quality's, I undertook to manage the cause, and was the principal disputant against God and piety, and for my performances received the applause of the whole company; upon which my mind was terribly struck, and I immediately replied thus to myself. Good God! that a man, that walks upright, that sees the wonderful works of God, and has the uses of his senses and reason, should use them to the defying of his Creator! But though this was a good beginning towards my conversion, to find my conscience touched for my sins, yet it went off again; nay, all my life long I had a secret value* and reverence for an honest man, and loved morality in others. But I had formed an odd scheme of religion to myself, which would solve all that God or Conscience *might force upon me; yet I was not ever well reconciled to the business of Christianity, nor had that reverence for the Gospel of Christ as I ought to have.* Which estate of mind continued, till the 53d Chapter of *Isaiah* was read to him, (wherein there is a lively description of the sufferings of our Saviour, and the benefits thereof,) and some other portions of Scripture; by the power and efficacy of which word, assisted by his holy Spirit, God so wrought upon his heart, that he declared that *the mysteries of the Passion appeared so clear and plain to him, as ever anything did that was represented in a glass.* . . .

Robert Parsons, *A Sermon preached at the Funeral of the Rt Honorable John Earl of Rochester*, Oxford, 1680, pp. 22–4

Plain Dealing's Downfall

[It has been suggested that Rochester composed this poem after hearing Parsons read from Isaiah, Chapter 53, of the Suffering Servant, 'despised and rejected of men'.]

> Long time Plain Dealing in the haughty town
> Wandering about, though in a threadbare gown,
> At last unanimously was cried down.
>
> When almost starved, she to the country fled,
> In hopes, though meanly, she should there be fed
> And tumble nightly on a pea-straw bed.
>
> But Knavery, knowing her intent, took post
> And rumoured her approach through every coast,
> Vowing his ruin that should be her host.
>
> Frighted at this, each rustic shut his door,
> Bid her be gone and trouble him no more,
> For he that entertained her must be poor.
>
> At this grief seized her, grief too great to tell,
> When weeping, sighing, fainting down she fell,
> Whilst Knavery, laughing, rung her passing bell.

'An Inward Force upon Him'

He said he was now persuaded both of the truth of Christianity and of the power of inward Grace, of which he gave me this strange account. He said Mr Parsons, in order to his conviction, read to him the 53 Chapter of the Prophecy of Isaiah and compared that with the history of our Saviour's Passion, that he might there see a prophecy concerning it written many ages before it was done; which the Jews that blasphemed Jesus Christ still kept in their hands as a book divinely inspired. He said to me that *as he heard it read he felt an inward force upon him, which did so enlighten his mind and convince him that he could resist it no longer: For the words had an authority which did shoot like rays or beams in his mind, so that he was not only convinced by the reasonings he had about it, which satisfied his understanding, but by a power which did so effectually constrain him that he did ever after as firmly believe in his Saviour as if he had seen him in the clouds.* He had made it be read so often to him that he had got it by heart: and went through a great part of it in discourse with me, with a sort of heavenly pleasure, giving me his reflections on it. Some few I remember, *Who hath believed our report? Here,* he said, *was foretold the opposition the Gospel was to meet with from such wretches as he was. He hath no form nor comeliness, and when we shall see him there is no beauty that we should desire him.* On this he said *The meanness of his appearance and person has made vain and foolish people disparage him because he came not in such a fool's coat as they delight in.* What he said on the other parts I do not well remember: and indeed I was so affected with what he said then to me that the general transport I was under during the whole discourse made me less capable to remember these particulars as I wish I had done.

Gilbert Burnet, *Some Passages of the Life and Death of the Right Honourable John Earl of Rochester,* London, 1680, pp. 140–3

His Old Guardian Receives the News

And now I must tell you some sad news. I much fear my Lord Rochester hath not long to live, he is here at his lodge & his mother my Lady Dowager and his lady are with him, and Doctor Short of London & Doctor Radcliffe of Oxon. Himself is now very weak, God Almighty restore him if it be His will, for he is grown to be the most altered person, the most devout & pious person as I generally ever knew, & certainly would make a most worthy brave man, if it would please God to spare his life, but I fear the worst, though there is hope while there is life & God Almighty is able to raise from the grave, but at present he is very weak & ill. But what gives us much comfort is we hope he will be happy in another world if it please God to take him hence.

And further what is much comfort to my Lady Dowager & us all in the midst of this sorrow is his lady is returned to her first love the Protestant religion and on Sunday last received the sacrament with her lord & hath been at prayer with us so as if it might please God to spare and restore him it would all together make up very great joy to my lady his mother & to us all that love him, but I shall trouble you no further but remain

Your most affectionate
& most humble servant,
John Cary.

June 1, 1680.
[To Sir Ralph Verney]

The Verney Papers, Claydon, Bucks.

Gilbert Burnet Writes to the Earl of Halifax

June 5th, 1680.

Will Fanshaw just now tells me letters are come from the Earl of Rochester, by which it seems he must be dead by this time. Dr Lowe is sent for, but they think he cannot live till he comes to him, an ulcer in his bladder is broken, and he pisses matter, he is in extreme pain: he has expressed great remorse for his past ill life and has persuaded his lady to receive the sacrament with him and hereafter to go to church and declare herself a Protestant, and dies a serious penitent and professes himself a Christian. Since Mr Fanshaw told me this I hear he is dead.

June 12th, 1680

The Earl of Rochester lives still and is in a probable way of recovering, for it is thought all that ulcerous matter is cast out; all the town is full of his great penitence, which, by your Lordship's good leave, I hope flows from a better principle than the height of his fancy, and indeed that which depends so much on the disposition of the body cannot be supposed very high when a man's spirits are so spent as his were. This, he told me in his last sickness, prevailed with him beyond all other arguments to think the soul was of a different nature from the body, for when he was so low that he could not stir, and thought not to live an hour, he had the free use of his reason to as high a degree as ever he remembered to have had in his whole life, but it was plain reason stript of fancy and conceit.

July 3rd, 1680.

I have had one of the best letters from the Earl of Rochester that ever I had from any person, he has a sedate and sincere repentance and a firm belief of the Christian religion deeply formed in his mind. He has little hopes of life and as little desires for it, unless that he may make amends for what is past.

July 29th, 1680.

I could not write to your Lordship on Saturday last, for it was late before I came home from the Earl of Rochester's, and having rid post and very hard, to which I have not been accustomed, was so uneasy that I could not write. Now I understand he died the night after I left him, though he did not think he was so near his end. His understanding was perfect and he had still the greatest flights of fancy that I ever knew in one so low. He was the greatest penitent I ever saw, and died a sincere Christian, but of this I shall say no more because he gave me in charge to publish an account how he died.

Camden Miscellany XI, pp. 32, 35, 36, 39, 41

John Cary to Sir Ralph Verney

(i)

June 15, 1680.

My Lord Rochester hath been ill a great while and continueth so still. He is advised to drink asses' milk and wants a good one that gives milk. My Lady his honourable mother presents her service to you and prays you if you have any such to lend it to her, or to procure one if you know of any thereabout, in which you will do his Lordship a great favour. . . .

Your most humble servant,
John Cary.

The Verney Papers, Claydon, Bucks.

(ii)

My Lord Rochester continues very weak & ill. I think he hath milch asses sufficient. . . .

Your most humble servant,
John Cary.

July 17, 1680.

I shall acquaint my Lord Rochester with your kind offer of a milch ass.

The Verney Papers, Claydon, Bucks.

Mr Fanshaw's Fright

When Wilmot Lord Rochester lay on his death-bed Mr Fanshaw came to visit him with an intention to stay about a week with him. Mr Fanshaw sitting by the bedside perceived his Lordp. praying to God through Jesus Christ, and acquainted Dr Radcliff (who attended my Lordp. in this illness and was then in the house) with what he had heard, and told him that my Lord was certainly delirious, for to his knowledge (he said) he believed neither in God nor Jesus Christ. The Dr (who had often heard him pray in the same manner) proposed to Mr F. to go up to his Ldp. to be further satisfied touching this affair. When they came to his room, the Dr told my Lord what Mr F. said. Upon which his Ldp. addressed himself to Mr F. to this effect: Sr. it is true you and I have been very lewd & profane together, and then I was of the opinion you mention; but now I am quite of another mind, & happy am I that I am so. I am very sensible how miserable I was whilst of another opinion. Sr. you may assure yourself that there is a judged future state, & so entered into a very handsome discourse concerning the Last Judgment, future states, etc. & concluded with a serious & pathetic exhortation to Mr F. to enter into another course of life, adding that he (Mr F.) knew him to be his friend, that he never was more so than at this time. And Sr. (said he), to use a Scripture expression, I am not mad, but speak the words of truth & soberness. Upon this, Mr F. trembled & went immediately afoot to Woodstock, & there hired a horse to Oxford and there took coach to London. At the same time Dr Shorter (who also attended my Lord in this illness) & Dr Radcliff walking together in the Park and discoursing touching his Ldp's condition, which they agreed to be past remedy, Dr Shorter, fetching a very deep sigh, said, 'Well, I can do him no good, but he has done me a great deal.' When Dr Radcliff came to reside in London he made enquiry about Dr Shorter & understood he was before that time a libertine in principles, but after that professed the Roman Catholic religion. I heard Dr Radcliff's accnt. at my Lord Oxford's table, (then Speaker of the House of Commons) June 16, 1702. Present (besides Mr Speaker) Ld. Weymouth, Mr Bromley of Warwickshire, Mr Wm. Harvey, Mr Pendarvis, Mr Hen. St John, & I wrote it down immediately.

Wm. Thomas.

British Museum, Harleian MS. 7003

'Even the Piggard-Boy'

In his last sickness he was exceedingly penitent and wrote a letter of his repentance to Dr Burnet, which is printed.

He sent for all his servants, even the piggard-boy, to come and hear his palinode. He died at Woodstock Park, 26 July, 1680; and buried at Spilsbury in the same county, Aug. 9 following.

John Aubrey, *Brief Lives*

'Has My Friend Left Me?'

I thought to have left him on Friday, but, not without some

passion, he desired me to stay that day: there appeared no symptom of present death; and a worthy physician then with him told me that though he was so low that an accident might carry him away on a sudden, yet without that he thought he might live yet some weeks. So on Saturday at four of the clock in the morning I left him, being the 24th of July. But I durst not take leave of him, for he had expressed so great an unwillingness to part with me the day before that if I had not presently yielded to one day's stay it was likely to have given him some trouble, therefore I thought it better to leave him without any formality. Some hours after he asked for me, and when it was told him I was gone, he seemed to be troubled and said, *Has my friend left me, then I shall die shortly*. After that he spake but once or twice till he died: He lay much silent: Once they heard him praying very devoutly. And on Monday, about two of the clock in the morning, he died, without any convulsion or so much as a groan.

Gilbert Burnet, *Some Passages of the Life and Death of the Right Honourable John Earl of Rochester*, London, 1680, pp. 156, 157

6

Epilogue (1685)

Sure there has not lived in many ages (if ever) so extraordinary, and, I think I may add, so useful a person as most Englishmen know my Lord to have been, whether we consider the constant good sense and the agreeable mirth of his ordinary conversation or the vast reach and compass of his invention and the wonderful depths of his retired thoughts, the uncommon graces of his fashion or the inimitable turns of his wit, the becoming gentleness, the bewitching softness of his civility or the force and fitness of his satire; for as he was both the delight and the wonder of men, the love and the dotage of women, so he was a continual curb to impertinence and the public censor of folly. Never did man stay in his company unentertained or leave it uninstructed; never was his understanding biassed or his pleasantness forced; never did he laugh in the wrong place or prostitute his sense to serve his luxury; never did he stab into the wounds of fallen virtue, with a base and cowardly insult, or smooth the face of prosperous villainy with the paint and washes of a mercenary wit; never did he spare a fop for being rich or flatter a knave for being great. As most men had an ambition (thinking it an indisputable title to wit) to be in the number of his friends, so few were his enemies, but such as did not know him or such as hated him for what others loved him, and never did he go among strangers but he gained admirers, if not friends, and commonly of such who had been before prejudiced against him. Never was his talk thought too much or his visit too long. . . .

He had a wit that was accompanied with an unaffected greatness of mind and a natural love to justice and truth; a wit that was in perpetual war with knavery and ever attacking those vices most whose malignity was like to be most diffusive, such as tended more immediately to the prejudice of public bodies and were of a common nuisance to the happiness of human kind. Never was his pen drawn but on the side of good sense, and usually imployed like the arms of the ancient heroes, to stop the progress of arbitrary oppression and beat down the brutishness of headstrong will; to do his King and Country justice upon such public State-thieves as would beggar a kingdom to enrich themselves, who, abusing the confidence and un-deserving the favour of a gracious Prince, will not be ashamed to maintain the cheating of their Master by the robbing and starving of their fellow-servants and under the best form of Government in the world blush not to live upon the spoil of others, till by their impudent violations of Right, they grow like beasts of prey, hostes humani generis. These were the vermin whom (to his eternal honour) his pen was continually pricking and goading. A pen if not so happy in the success as generous in the aim, as either the sword of Theseus or the club of Hercules; nor was it less sharp than that or less weighty than this. If he did not take so much care of himself as he ought, he had the humanity, however, to wish well to others, and I think I may truly affirm, he did the world as much good by the right application of satire as he hurt himself by a wrong pursuit of pleasure.

> Preface by 'one of his friends' (i.e. Robert Wolseley) to *Valentinian: a Tragedy. As 'tis Altered by the late Earl of Rochester and Acted at the Theatre Royal*, London, 1685. The part of Lucina was acted by another of his friends, Elizabeth Barry.

NOTES

1 Robert Plot, *The Natural History of Oxfordshire*, Oxford, 1677, pp. 7–15.
2 F. R. Leavis, *Revaluation*, London, 1936, p. 35.
3 Wilhelm Reich, *The Function of the Orgasm*, New York, 1961, p. 204.
4 Anne Righter, *John Wilmot Earl of Rochester* (Chatterton Lecture on an English Poet), London, 1967, p. 69.
5 Gilbert Burnet, *Some Passages of the Life and Death of the Right Honourable John Earl of Rochester*, London, 1680, pp. 38, 39.
6 Burnet, *Some Passages*, p. 110.
7 Burnet, *Some Passages*, p. 40.
8 Burnet, *Some Passages*, p. 41.
9 Burnet, *Some Passages*, p. 8.
10 Part I, Chapter 4 (Pelican Classics edition, p. 108).
11 Robert Parsons, *A Sermon Preached at the Funeral of the Right Honorable John Earl of Rochester*, Oxford, 1680, p. 26.
12 Similarly, in 'A Satire against Reason and Mankind' 'ignis fatuus' is Reason, whereas in *Leviathan*, Part I, Chapter 5, 'metaphors and senseless and ambiguous words are like *ignes fatui*; and reasoning upon them is wandering . . .' (Pelican Classics edition, pp. 116, 117).
13 Part I, Chapter 3 (Pelican Classics edition, p. 97). This same chapter seems to have given Dryden the image of the spaniel in the Prefaces to *Annus Mirabilis* and *The Rival Ladies*.
14 'This livelong minute' recalls 'the lucky minute' in 'Song' ('As Chloris full of harmless thoughts . . .') and 'the happy minute' in 'Song' ('Fair Chloris in a pigsty lay, . . .'). There is also the 'happy minute' of the song in Dryden's *Cleomenes*.
15 Ronald Berman, 'Rochester and the Defeat of the Senses', *Kenyon Review*, Spring 1964, p. 357.
16 Berman, in *Kenyon Review*, Spring 1964, p. 365.
17 It is the subject of poems by Waller, Cartwright, Aurelian Townshend, all to be found, together with this poem by Rochester, in Dame Helen Gardner's *The Metaphysical Poets* (Penguin).
18 J. H. Wilson, *The Court Wits of the Restoration*, Princeton, 1948, p. 85.
19 'The Imperfect Enjoyment'.

20 'A Ramble in St James's Park'.
21 David Vieth, *Complete Poems of John Wilmot, Earl of Rochester*, New Haven and London, 1968, p. vi.
22 Rodney M. Baine, 'Rochester or Fishbourne: A Question of Authorship', *Review of English Studies*, 22, pp. 201–6.
23 Francis Hall, otherwise Line, S. J., *An Explanation of the Dial set up in the King's Garden at London*, Liège, 1673, p. 52. This volume contains the drawing referred to.
24 'The Advice'.
25 Burnet, *Some Passages*, p. 7.
26 Burnet, *Some Passages*, p. 13.
27 Righter, *John Wilmot Earl of Rochester*, pp. 63–4.
28 Vieth, *Complete Poems of John Wilmot, Earl of Rochester*, p. xxxvii.
29 Burnet, *Some Passages*, p. 28.
30 Burnet, *Some Passages*, p. 159.